Introduction to Compilers and Language Design

Prof. Douglas Thain
University of Notre Dame

For Lisa, William, Zachary, Emily, and Alia.

Contributions

I am grateful to the following people for their contributions to this book:

Andrew Litteken drafted the chapter on ARM assembly; Kevin Latimer drew the RegEx to NFA and the LR example figures; Benjamin Gunning fixed an error in LL(1) parse table construction; Tim Shaffer completed the detailed LR(1) example.

And the following people corrected typos:
John Westhoff (25), Gonzalo Martinez (25), Daniel Kerrigan (24), Brian DuSell (23), Ryan Mackey (20), Nedim Mininovic (15), Joseph Kimlinger (12), Andrew Litteken (9), Thomas Cane (9), Stéphane Massou (8), Luis Prieb (7), Jonathan Xu (6), John Johnson (4), Spencer King (2), Yaoxian Qu (2), Maria Aranguren (2), Patrick Lacher (2), Connor Higgins (2), Tango Gu (2), Andrew Syrmakesis (2), Horst von Brand (2), Benjamin Gunning (1) Charles Osborne (1), William Theisen (1), Jessica Cioffi (1), Ben Tovar (1), Ryan Michalec (1), Patrick Flynn (1), Clint Jeffery (1), Ralph Siemsen (1)

Please send any comments or corrections via email to Prof. Douglas Thain (dthain@nd.edu).

Contents

List of Figures

Chapter 1 – Introduction

1.1 What is a compiler?

A **compiler** translates a program in a **source language** to a program in a **target language**. The most well known form of a compiler is one that translates a high level language like C into the native assembly language of a machine so that it can be executed. And of course there are compilers for other languages like C++, Java, C#, and Rust, and many others.

The same techniques used in a traditional compiler are also used in any kind of program that processes a language. For example, a typesetting program like TEX translates a manuscript into a Postscript document. A graph-layout program like Dot consumes a list of nodes and edges and arranges them on a screen. A web browser translates an HTML document into an interactive graphical display. To write programs like these, you need to understand and use the same techniques as in traditional compilers.

Compilers exist not only to *translate* programs, but also to *improve* them. A compiler assists a programmer by finding errors in a program at compile time, so that the user does not have to encounter them at runtime. Usually, a more strict language results in more compile-time errors. This makes the programmer's job harder, but makes it more likely that the program is correct. For example, the Ada language is infamous among programmers as challenging to write without compile-time errors, but once working, is trusted to run safety-critical systems such as the Boeing 777 aircraft.

A compiler is distinct from an **interpreter**, which reads in a program and then executes it directly, without emitting a translation. This is also sometimes known as a **virtual machine** Languages like Python and Ruby are typically executed by an interpreter that reads the source code directly.

Compilers and interpreters are closely related, and it is sometimes possible to exchange one for the other. For example, Java compilers translate Java source code into Java **bytecode**, which is an abstract form of assembly language. Some implementations of the Java Virtual Machine work as interpreters that execute one instruction at a time. Others work by translating the bytecode into local machine code, and then running the machine code directly. This is known as **just in time compiling** or **JIT**.

1.2   Why should you study compilers?

You will be a better programmer. A great craftsman must understand his or her tools, and a programmer is no different. By understanding more deeply how a compiler translates your program into machine language, you will become more skilled at writing effective code and debugging it when things go wrong.

You can create tools for debugging and translating. If you can write a parser for a given language, then you can write all manner of supporting tools that help you (and others) debug your own programs. An integrated development environment like Eclipse incorporates parsers for languages like Java, so that it can highlight syntax, find errors without compiling, and connect code to documentation as you write.

You can create new languages. A surprising number of problems are made easier by expressing them compactly in a custom language. (These are sometimes known as **domain specific languages** or simply **little languages**.) By learning the techniques of compilers, you will be able to implement little languages and avoid some pitfalls of language design.

You can contribute to existing compilers. While it's unlikely that you will write the next great C compiler (since we already have several), language and compiler development does not stand still. Standards development results in new language features; optimization research creates new ways of improving programs; new microprocessors are created; new operating systems are developed; and so on. All of these developments require the continuous improvement of existing compilers.

You will have fun while solving challenging problems. Isn't that enough?

1.3   What's the best way to learn about compilers?

The best way to learn about compilers is to *write your own compiler* from beginning to end. While that may sound daunting at first, you will find that this complex task can be broken down into several stages of moderate complexity. The typical undergraduate computer science student can write a complete compiler for a simple language in a semester, broken down into four or five independent stages.

1.4   What language should I use?

Without question, you should use the C programming language and the X86 assembly language, of course!

Ok, maybe the answer isn't quite that simple. There is an ever-increasing number of programming languages that all have different strengths and weaknesses. Java is simple, consistent, and portable, albeit not high performance. Python is easy to learn and has great library support, but weak typing. Rust offers exceptional static type-safety, but is not (yet) widely used. It is quite possible to write a compiler in nearly any language, and you could use this book as a guide to do so.

However, we really think that you should learn C, write a compiler in C, and use it to compile a C-like language which produces assembly for a widely-used processor, like X86 or ARM. Why? Because it is important for you to learn the ins and outs of technologies that are in wide use, and not just those that are abstractly beautiful.

C is the most widely-used portable language for low-level coding (compilers, and libraries, and kernels) and it is also small enough that one can learn how to compile every aspect of C in a single semester. True, C presents some challenges related to type safety and pointer use, but these are manageable for a project the size of a compiler. There are other languages with different virtues, but none as simple and as widely used as C. Once you write a C compiler, then you are free to design your own (better) language.

Likewise, the X86 has been the most widely-deployed computer architecture in desktops, servers, and laptops for several decades. While it is considerably more complex than other architectures like MIPS or SPARC or ARM, one can quickly learn the essential subset of instructions necessary to build a compiler. Of course, ARM is quickly catching up as a popular architecture in the mobile, embedded, and low power space, so we have included a section on that as well.

That said, the principles presented in this book are widely applicable. If you are using this as part of a class, your instructor may very well choose a different compilation language and different target assembly, and that's fine too.

1.5 How is this book different from others?

Most books on compilers are very heavy on the abstract theory of scanners, parsers, type systems, and register allocation, and rather light on how the design of a language affects the compiler and the runtime. Most are designed for use by a graduate survey of optimization techniques.

This book takes a broader approach by giving a lighter dose of optimization, and introducing more material on the process of engineering a compiler, the tradeoffs in language design, and considerations for interpretation and translation.

You will also notice that this book doesn't contain a whole bunch of fiddly paper-and-pencil assignments to test your knowledge of compiler algorithms. (Ok, there are a few of those in Chapters 3 and 4.) If you want to test your knowledge, then write some working code. To that end, the exercises at the end of each chapter ask you to take the ideas in the chapter, and either explore some existing compilers, or write parts of your own. If you do all of them in order, you will end up with a working compiler, summarized in the final appendix.

1.6   What other books should I read?

For general reference on compilers, I suggest the following books:

- **Charles N. Fischer, Ron K. Cytron, and Richard J. LeBlanc Jr, "Crafting a Compiler", Pearson, 2009.**
  This is an excellent undergraduate textbook which focuses on object-oriented software engineering techniques for constructing a compiler, with a focus on generating output for the Java Virtual Machine.

- **Christopher Fraser and David Hanson, "A Retargetable C Compiler: Design and Implementation", Benjamin/Cummings, 1995.**
  Also known as the "LCC book", this book focuses entirely on explaining the C implementation of a C compiler by taking the unusual approach of embedding the literal code into the textbook, so that code and explanation are intertwined.

- **Alfred V. Aho, Monica S. Lam, Ravi Sethi, and Jeffrey D. Ullman, "Compilers: Principles, Techniques, and Tools", Addison Wesley, 2006.** *Affectionately known as the "dragon book", this is a comprehensive treatment of the theory of compilers from scanning through type theory and optimization at an advanced graduate level.*

Ok, what are you waiting for? Let's get to work.

Chapter 2 – A Quick Tour

2.1 The Compiler Toolchain

A compiler is one component in a **toolchain** of programs used to create executables from source code. Typically, when you invoke a single command to compile a program, a whole sequence of programs are invoked in the background. Figure 2.1 shows the programs typically used in a Unix system for compiling C source code to assembly code.

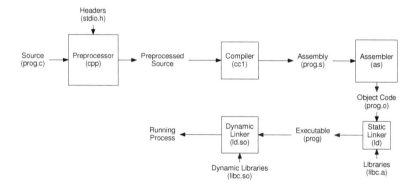

Figure 2.1: A Typical Compiler Toolchain

- The **preprocessor** prepares the source code for the compiler proper. In the C and C++ languages, this means consuming all directives that start with the # symbol. For example, an #include directive causes the pre-processor to open the named file and insert its contents into the source code. A #define directive causes the preprocessor to substitute a value wherever a macro name is encountered. (Not all languages rely on a preprocessor.)

- The **compiler** proper consumes the clean output of the preprocessor. It scans and parses the source code, performs typechecking and other semantic routines, optimizes the code, and then produces assembly language as the output. This part of the toolchain is the main focus of this book.

- The **assembler** consumes the assembly code and produces **object code**. Object code is "almost executable" in that it contains raw machine language instructions in the form needed by the CPU. However, object code does not know the final memory addresses in which it will be loaded, and so it contains gaps that must be filled in by the linker.

- The **linker** consumes one or more object files and library files and combines them into a complete, executable program. It selects the final memory locations where each piece of code and data will be loaded, and then "links" them together by writing in the missing address information. For example, an object file that calls the `printf` function does not initially know the address of the function. An empty (zero) address will be left where the address must be used. Once the linker selects the memory location of `printf`, it must go back and write in the address at every place where `printf` is called.

In Unix-like operating systems, the preprocessor, compiler, assembler, and linker are historically named `cpp`, `cc1`, `as`, and `ld` respectively. The user-visible program `cc` simply invokes each element of the toolchain in order to produce the final executable.

2.2   Stages Within a Compiler

In this book, our focus will be primarily on the compiler proper, which is the most interesting component in the toolchain. The compiler itself can be divided into several stages:

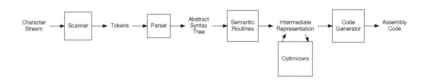

Figure 2.2: The Stages of a Unix Compiler

- The **scanner** consumes the plain text of a program, and groups together individual characters to form complete **tokens**. This is much like grouping characters into words in a natural language.

- The **parser** consumes tokens and groups them together into complete statements and expressions, much like words are grouped into sentences in a natural language. The parser is guided by a **grammar** which states the formal rules of composition in a given language. The output of the parser is an **abstract syntax tree (AST)** that captures the grammatical structures of the program. The AST also remembers where in the source file each construct appeared, so it is able to generate targeted error messages, if needed.

- The **semantic routines** traverse the AST and derive additional meaning (semantics) about the program from the rules of the language and the relationship between elements of the program. For example, we might determine that x + 10 is a float expression by observing the type of x from an earlier declaration, then applying the language rule that addition between int and float values yields a float. After the semantic routines, the AST is often converted into an **intermediate representation (IR)** which is a simplified form of assembly code suitable for detailed analysis. There are many forms of IR which we will discuss in Chapter 8.

- One or more **optimizers** can be applied to the intermediate representation, in order to make the program smaller, faster, or more efficient. Typically, each optimizer reads the program in IR format, and then emits the same IR format, so that each optimizer can be applied independently, in arbitrary order.

- Finally, a **code generator** consumes the optimized IR and transforms it into a concrete assembly language program. Typically, a code generator must perform **register allocation** to effectively manage the limited number of hardware registers, and **instruction selection** and **sequencing** to order assembly instructions in the most efficient form.

2.3 Example Compilation

Suppose we wish to compile this fragment of code into assembly:

```
height = (width+56) * factor(foo)
```

The first stage of the compiler (the scanner) will read in the text of the source code character by character, identify the boundaries between symbols, and emit a series of **tokens**. Each token is a small data structure that describes the nature and contents of each symbol:

| id:height | = | (| id:width | + | int:56 |) | * | id:factor | (| id:foo |) | ; |

At this stage, the purpose of each token is not yet clear. For example, factor and foo are simply known to be identifiers, even though one is the name of a function, and the other is the name of a variable. Likewise, we do not yet know the type of `width`, so the + could potentially represent integer addition, floating point addition, string concatenation, or something else entirely.

The next step is to determine whether this sequence of tokens forms a valid program. The parser does this by looking for patterns that match the **grammar** of a language. Suppose that our compiler understands a language with the following grammar:

Grammar G$_1$

1. expr → expr + expr
2. expr → expr * expr
3. expr → expr = expr
4. expr → id (expr)
5. expr → (expr)
6. expr → id
7. expr → int

Each line of the grammar is called a rule, and explains how various parts of the language are constructed. Rules 1-3 indicate that an expression can be formed by joining two expressions with operators. Rule 4 describes a function call. Rule 5 describes the use of parentheses. Finally, rules 6 and 7 indicate that identifiers and integers are atomic expressions. [1]

The parser looks for sequences of tokens that can be replaced by the left side of a rule in our grammar. Each time a rule is applied, the parser creates a node in a tree, and connects the sub-expressions into the **abstract syntax tree (AST)**. The AST shows the structural relationships between each symbol: addition is performed on `width` and `56`, while a function call is applied to `factor` and `foo`.

With this data structure in place, we are now prepared to analyze the meaning of the program. The **semantic routines** traverse the AST and derive additional meaning by relating parts of the program to each other, and to the definition of the programming language. An important component of this process is **typechecking**, in which the type of each expression is determined, and checked for consistency with the rest of the program. To keep things simple here, we will assume that all of our variables are plain integers.

To generate linear intermediate code, we perform a post-order traversal of the AST and generate an IR instruction for each node in the tree. A typical IR looks like an abstract assembly language, with load/store instructions, arithmetic operations, and an infinite number of registers. For example, this is a possible IR representation of our example program:

---

[1]The careful reader will note that this example grammar has ambiguities. We will discuss that in some detail in Chapter 4.

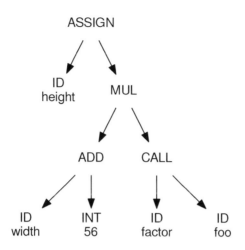

Figure 2.3: Example AST

```
LOAD $56      -> r1
LOAD width    -> r2
IADD r1, r2   -> r3
PUSH foo
CALL factor   -> r4
IMUL r3, r4   -> r5
STOR r6       -> height
```

Figure 2.4: Example Intermediate Representation

The intermediate representation is where most forms of optimization occur. Dead code is removed, common operations are combined, and code is generally simplified to consume fewer resources and run more quickly.

Finally, the intermediate code must be converted to the desired assembly code. Figure 2.5 shows X86 assembly code that is one possible translation of the IR given above. Note that the assembly instructions do not necessarily correspond one-to-one with IR instructions.

A well-engineered compiler is highly modular, so that common code elements can be shared and combined as needed. To support multiple languages, a compiler can provide distinct scanners and parsers, each emitting the same intermediate representation. Different optimization techniques can be implemented as independent modules (each reading and

```
MOVL    width, %eax      # load width into eax
ADDL    $56, %eax        # add 56 to eax
MOVL    %eax, -8(%rbp)   # save sum in temporary
MOVL    foo, %edi        # load foo into arg 0 register
CALL    factor           # invoke function
MOVL    -8(%rbp), %edx   # recover sum from temporary
IMULL   %eax, %edx       # multiply them together
MOVL    %edx, height     # store result into height
```

Figure 2.5: Example Assembly Code

writing the same IR) so that they can be enabled and disable independently. A retargetable compiler contains multiple code generators, so that the same IR can be emitted for a variety of microprocessors.

2.4   Exercises

1. Determine how to invoke the preprocessor, compiler, assembler, and linker manually in your local computing environment. Compile a small complete program that computes a simple expression, and examine the output at each stage. Are you able to follow the flow of the program in each form?

2. Determine how to change the optimization level for your local compiler. Find a non-trivial source program and compile it at multiple levels of optimization. How does the compile time, program size, and run time vary with optimization levels?

3. Search the internet for the formal grammars for three languages that you are familiar with, such as C++, Ruby, and Rust. Compare them side by side. Which language is inherently more complex? Do they share any common structures?

Chapter 3 – Scanning

3.1 Kinds of Tokens

Scanning is the process of identifying **tokens** from the raw text source code of a program. At first glance, scanning might seem trivial – after all, identifying words in a natural language is as simple as looking for spaces between letters. However, identifying tokens in source code requires the language designer to clarify many fine details, so that it is clear what is permitted and what is not.

Most languages will have tokens in these categories:

- **Keywords** are words in the language structure itself, like `while` or `class` or `true`. Keywords must be chosen carefully to reflect the natural structure of the language, without interfering with the likely names of variables and other identifiers.

- **Identifiers** are the names of variables, functions, classes, and other code elements chosen by the programmer. Typically, identifiers are arbitrary sequences of letters and possibly numbers. Some languages require identifiers to be marked with a **sentinel** (like the dollar sign in Perl) to clearly distinguish identifiers from keywords.

- **Numbers** could be formatted as integers, or floating point values, or fractions, or in alternate bases such as binary, octal or hexadecimal. Each format should be clearly distinguished, so that the programmer does not confuse one with the other.

- **Strings** are literal character sequences that must be clearly distinguished from keywords or identifiers. Strings are typically quoted with single or double quotes, but also must have some facility for containing quotations, newlines, and unprintable characters.

- **Comments** and **whitespace** are used to format a program to make it visually clear, and in some cases (like Python) are significant to the structure of a program.

When designing a new language, or designing a compiler for an existing language, the first job is to state precisely what characters are permitted in each type of token. Initially, this could be done informally by stating,

```
token_t scan_token( FILE *fp ) {
    int c = fgetc(fp);
    if(c=='*') {
        return TOKEN_MULTIPLY;
    } else if(c=='!') {
        char d = fgetc(fp);
        if(d=='=') {
            return TOKEN_NOT_EQUAL;
        } else {
            ungetc(d,fp);
            return TOKEN_NOT;
        }
    } else if(isalpha(c)) {
        do {
            char d = fgetc(fp);
        } while(isalnum(d));
        ungetc(d,fp);
        return TOKEN_IDENTIFIER;
    } else if ( . . . ) {
        . . .
    }
}
```

Figure 3.1: A Simple Hand Made Scanner

for example, *"An identifier consists of a letter followed by any number of letters and numerals."*, and then assigning a symbolic constant (TOKEN_IDENTIFIER) for that kind of token. As we will see, an informal approach is often ambiguous, and a more rigorous approach is needed.

3.2   A Hand-Made Scanner

Figure 3.1 shows how one might write a scanner by hand, using simple coding techniques. To keep things simple, we only consider just a few tokens: * for multiplication, ! for logical-not, != for not-equal, and sequences of letters and numbers for identifiers.

The basic approach is to read one character at a time from the input stream (fgetc(fp)) and then classify it. Some single-character tokens are easy: if the scanner reads a * character, it immediately returns TOKEN_MULTIPLY, and the same would be true for addition, subtraction, and so forth.

However, some characters are part of multiple tokens. If the scanner encounters !, that could represent a logical-not operation by itself, or it could be the first character in the != sequence representing not-equal-to. Upon reading !, the scanner must immediately read the next character. If

the next character is =, then it has matched the sequence != and returns
TOKEN_NOT_EQUAL.

But, if the character following ! is something else, then the non-matching
character needs to be *put back* on the input stream using ungetc, because
it is not part of the current token. The scanner returns TOKEN_NOT and will
consume the put-back character on the next call to scan_token.

In a similar way, once a letter has been identified by isalpha(c), then
the scanner keeps reading letters or numbers, until a non-matching character is found. The non-matching character is put back, and the scanner
returns TOKEN_IDENTIFIER.

(We will see this pattern come up in every stage of the compiler: an
unexpected item doesn't match the current objective, so it must be put
back for later. This is known more generally as **backtracking**.)

As you can see, a hand-made scanner is rather verbose. As more token types are added, the code can become quite convoluted, particularly
if tokens share common sequences of characters. It can also be difficult
for a developer to be certain that the scanner code corresponds to the desired definition of each token, which can result in unexpected behavior on
complex inputs. That said, for a small language with a limited number of
tokens, a hand-made scanner can be an appropriate solution.

For a complex language with a large number of tokens, we need a more
formalized approach to defining and scanning tokens. A formal approach
will allow us to have a greater confidence that token definitions do not
conflict and the scanner is implemented correctly. Further, a formalized
approach will allow us to make the scanner compact and high performance – surprisingly, the scanner itself can be the performance bottleneck
in a compiler, since every single character must be individually considered.

The formal tools of **regular expressions** and **finite automata** allow us
to state very precisely what may appear in a given token type. Then, automated tools can process these definitions, find errors or ambiguities, and
produce compact, high performance code.

3.3 Regular Expressions

Regular expressions (REs) are a language for expressing patterns. They
were first described in the 1950s by Stephen Kleene [4] as an element of
his foundational work in automata theory and computability. Today, REs
are found in slightly different forms in programming languages (Perl),
standard libraries (PCRE), text editors (vi), command-line tools (grep),
and many other places. We can use regular expressions as a compact
and formal way of specifying the tokens accepted by the scanner of a
compiler, and then automatically translate those expressions into working
code. While easily explained, REs can be a bit tricky to use, and require
some practice in order to achieve the desired results.

Let us define regular expressions precisely:

A **regular expression** s is a string which denotes $L(s)$, a set of strings drawn from an alphabet Σ. $L(s)$ is known as the "language of s."

$L(s)$ is defined inductively with the following base cases:

- If $a \in \Sigma$ then a is a regular expression and $L(a) = \{a\}$.

- ϵ is a regular expression and $L(\epsilon)$ contains only the empty string.

Then, for any regular expressions s and t:

1. $s|t$ is a RE such that $L(s|t) = L(s) \cup L(t)$.

2. st is a RE such that $L(st)$ contains all strings formed by the concatenation of a string in $L(s)$ followed by a string in $L(t)$.

3. s^* is a RE such that $L(s^*) = L(s)$ concatenated zero or more times.

Rule #3 is known as the **Kleene closure** and has the highest precedence. Rule #2 is known as **concatenation**. Rule #1 has the lowest precedence and is known as **alternation**. Parentheses can be added to adjust the order of operations in the usual way.

Here are a few examples using just the basic rules. (Note that a finite RE can indicate an infinite set.)

Regular Expression s	Language L(s)
`hello`	{ `hello` }
`d(o|i)g`	{ `dog,dig` }
`moo*`	{ `mo,moo,mooo, ...` }
`(moo)*`	{ `ε,moo,moomoo,moomoomoo, ...` }
`a(b|a)*a`	{ `aaa,aba,aaaa,aaba,abaa,abba, ...` }

The syntax described on the previous page is entirely sufficient to write any regular expression. But, is it also handy to have a few helper operations built on top of the basic syntax:

> `s?` indicates that `s` is optional.
> `s?` can be written as `(s|ε)`
>
> `s+` indicates that `s` is repeated one or more times.
> `s+` can be written as `ss*`
>
> `[a-z]` indicates any character in that range.
> `[a-z]` can be written as `(a|b| ... |z)`
>
> `[^x]` indicates any character except one.
> `[^x]` can be written as Σ - x

Regular expressions also obey several algebraic properties, which make it possible to re-arrange them as needed for efficiency or clarity:

Associativity:	`a|(b|c) = (a|b)|c`
Commutativity:	`a|b = b|a`
Distribution:	`a(b|c) = ab|ac`
Idempotency:	`a** = a*`

Using regular expressions, we can precisely state what is permitted in a given token. Suppose we have a hypothetical programming language with the following informal definitions and regular expressions. For each token type, we show examples of strings that match (and do not match) the regular expression.

Informal definition:	*An identifier is a sequence of capital letters and numbers, but a number must not come first.*
Regular expression:	`[A-Z]+([A-Z]|[0-9])*`
Matches strings:	`PRINT`
	`MODE5`
Does not match:	`hello`
	`4YOU`

Informal definition:	*A number is a sequence of digits with an optional decimal point. For clarity, the decimal point must have digits on both left and right sides.*
Regular expression:	`[0-9]+(.[0-9]+)?`
Matches strings:	`123`
	`3.14`
Does not match:	`.15`
	`30.`

Informal definition:	*A comment is any text (except a right angle bracket) surrounded by angle brackets.*
Regular expression:	`<[^>]*>`
Matches strings:	`<tricky part>`
	`<<<<look left>`
Does not match:	`<this is an <illegal> comment>`

3.4 Finite Automata

A **finite automaton (FA)** is an abstract machine that can be used to represent certain forms of computation. Graphically, an FA consists of a number of states (represented by numbered circles) and a number of edges (represented by labelled arrows) between those states. Each edge is labelled with one or more symbols drawn from an alphabet Σ.

The machine begins in a start state S_0. For each input symbol presented to the FA, it moves to the state indicated by the edge with the same label

as the input symbol. Some states of the FA are known as **accepting states**
and are indicated by a double circle. If the FA is in an accepting state after
all input is consumed, then we say that the FA **accepts** the input. We say
that the FA **rejects** the input string if it ends in a non-accepting state, or if
there is no edge corresponding to the current input symbol.

Every RE can be written as an FA, and vice versa. For a simple regular
expression, one can construct an FA by hand. For example, here is an FA
for the keyword `for`:

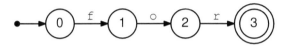

Here is an FA for identifiers of the form `[a-z][a-z0-9]+`

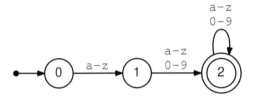

And here is an FA for numbers of the form `([1-9][0-9]*)|0`

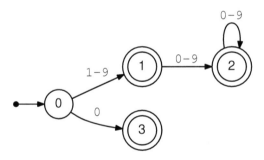

3.4.1 Deterministic Finite Automata

Each of these three examples is a **deterministic finite automaton** (DFA).
A DFA is a special case of an FA where every state has no more than one
outgoing edge for a given symbol. Put another way, a DFA has no ambiguity: for every combination of state and input symbol, there is exactly
one choice of what to do next.

Because of this property, a DFA is very easy to implement in software
or hardware. One integer (c) is needed to keep track of the current state.

The transitions between states are represented by a matrix ($M[s, i]$) which encodes the next state, given the current state and input symbol. (If the transition is not allowed, we mark it with E to indicate an error.) For each symbol, we compute $c = M[s, i]$ until all the input is consumed, or an error state is reached.

3.4.2 Nondeterministic Finite Automata

The alternative to a DFA is a **nondeterministic finite automaton (NFA)**. An NFA is a perfectly valid FA, but it has an ambiguity that makes it somewhat more difficult to work with.

Consider the regular expression [a-z]*ing, which represents all lowercase words ending in the suffix ing. It can be represented with the following automaton:

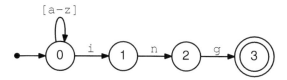

Now consider how this automaton would consume the word sing. It could proceed in two different ways. One would be to move to state 0 on s, state 1 on i, state 2 on n, and state 3 on g. But the other, equally valid way would be to stay in state 0 the whole time, matching each letter to the [a-z] transition. Both ways obey the transition rules, but one results in acceptance, while the other results in rejection.

The problem here is that state 0 allows for two different transitions on the symbol i. One is to stay in state 0 matching [a-z] and the other is to move to state 1 matching i.

Moreover, there is no simple rule by which we can pick one path or another. If the input is sing, the right solution is to proceed immediately from state zero to state one on i. But if the input is singing, then we should stay in state zero for the first ing and proceed to state one for the second ing

An NFA can also have an ϵ (epsilon) transition, which represents the empty string. This transition can be taken without consuming any input symbols at all. For example, we could represent the regular expression a*(ab|ac) with this NFA:

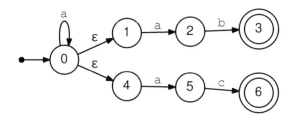

This particular NFA presents a variety of ambiguous choices. From state zero, it could consume a and stay in state zero. Or, it could take an ϵ to state one or state four, and then consume an a either way.

There are two common ways to interpret this ambiguity:

- The **crystal ball interpretation** suggests that the NFA somehow "knows" what the best choice is, by some means external to the NFA itself. In the example above, the NFA would choose whether to proceed to state zero, one, or four before consuming the first character, and it would always make the right choice. Needless to say, this isn't possible in a real implementation.

- The **many-worlds interpretation** suggests that that NFA exists in all allowable states *simultaneously*. When the input is complete, if any of those states are accepting states, then the NFA has accepted the input. This interpretation is more useful for constructing a working NFA, or converting it to a DFA.

Let us use the many-worlds interpretation on the example above. Suppose that the input string is aaac. Initially the NFA is in state zero. Without consuming any input, it could take an epsilon transition to states one or four. So, we can consider its initial state to be all of those states simultaneously. Continuing on, the NFA would traverse these states until accepting the complete string aaac:

States	Action
0, 1, 4	consume a
0, 1, 2, 4, 5	consume a
0, 1, 2, 4, 5	consume a
0, 1, 2, 4, 5	consume c
6	accept

In principle, one can implement an NFA in software or hardware by simply keeping track of all of the possible states. But this is inefficient. In the worst case, we would need to evaluate all states for all characters on each input transition. A better approach is to convert the NFA into an equivalent DFA, as we show below.

3.5 Conversion Algorithms

Regular expressions and finite automata are all equally powerful. For every RE, there is an FA, and vice versa. However, a DFA is by far the most straightforward of the three to implement in software. In this section, we will show how to convert an RE into an NFA, then an NFA into a DFA, and then to optimize the size of the DFA.

Figure 3.2: Relationship Between REs, NFAs, and DFAs

3.5.1 Converting REs to NFAs

To convert a regular expression to a nondeterministic finite automata, we can follow an algorithm given first by McNaughton and Yamada [5], and then by Ken Thompson [6].

We follow the same inductive definition of regular expression as given earlier. First, we define automata corresponding to the base cases of REs:

The NFA for any character a is: The NFA for an ϵ transition is:

Now, suppose that we have already constructed NFAs for the regular expressions A and B, indicated below by rectangles. Both A and B have a single start state (on the left) and accepting state (on the right). If we write the concatenation of A and B as AB, then the corresponding NFA is simply A and B connected by an ϵ transition. The start state of A becomes the start state of the combination, and the accepting state of B becomes the accepting state of the combination:

The NFA for the concatenation AB is:

In a similar fashion, the alternation of A and B written as A | B an be expressed as two automata joined by common starting and accepting nodes, all connected by ϵ transitions:

The NFA for the alternation A | B is:

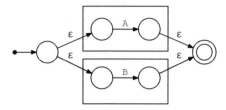

Finally, the Kleene closure A* is constructed by taking the automaton for A, adding starting and accepting nodes, then adding ϵ transitions to allow zero or more repetitions:

The NFA for the Kleene closure A* is:

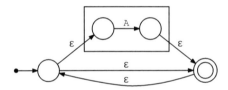

Example. Let's consider the process for an example regular expression a(cat | cow) *. First, we start with the innermost expression cat and assemble it into three transitions resulting in an accepting state. Then, do the same thing for cow, yielding these two FAs:

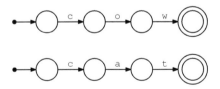

The alternation of the two expressions cat | cow is accomplished by adding a new starting and accepting node, with epsilon transitions. (The boxes are not part of the graph, but simply highlight the previous graph components carried forward.)

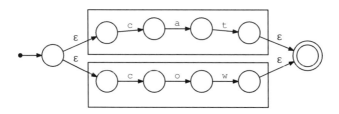

Then, the Kleene closure (cat | cow) * is accomplished by adding another starting and accepting state around the previous FA, with epsilon transitions between:

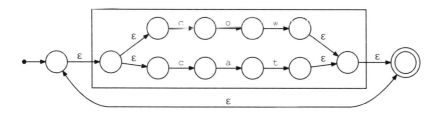

Finally, the concatenation of a (cat | cow) * is achieved by adding a single state at the beginning for a: smaller pieces:

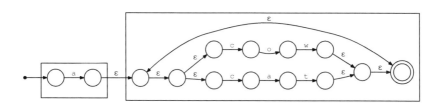

You can easily see that the NFA resulting from the construction algorithm, while correct, is quite complex and contains a large number of epsilon transitions. An NFA representing the tokens for a complete language could end up having thousands of states, which would be very impractical to implement. Instead, we can convert this NFA into an equivalent DFA.

3.5.2   Converting NFAs to DFAs

We can convert any NFA into an equivalent DFA using the technique of
subset construction. The basic idea is to create a DFA such that each state
in the DFA corresponds to multiple states in the NFA, according to the
"many-worlds" interpretation.

Suppose that we begin with an NFA consisting of states N and start
state N_0. We wish to construct an equivalent DFA consisting of states D
and start state D_0. Each D state will correspond to multiple N states. First,
we define a helper function known as the **epsilon closure**:

Epsilon closure.
$\epsilon-$closure(n) is the set of NFA states reachable from NFA state n by zero
or more ϵ transitions.

Now we define the subset construction algorithm. First, we create a
start state D_0 corresponding to the $\epsilon-$closure(N_0). Then, for each outgoing character c from the states in D_0, we create a new state containing the
epsilon closure of the states reachable by c. More precisely:

Subset Construction Algorithm.
Given an NFA with states N and start state N_0, create an equivalent DFA
with states D and start state D_0.

Let $D_0 = \epsilon-$closure(N_0).
Add D_0 to a list.
While items remain on the list:
       Let d be the next DFA state removed from the list.
       For each character c in Σ:
              Let T contain all NFA states N_k such that:
                  $N_j \in d$ and $N_j \xrightarrow{c} N_k$
              Create new DFA state $D_i = \epsilon-$closure(T)
              If D_i is not already in the list, add it to the end.

Figure 3.3: Subset Construction Algorithm

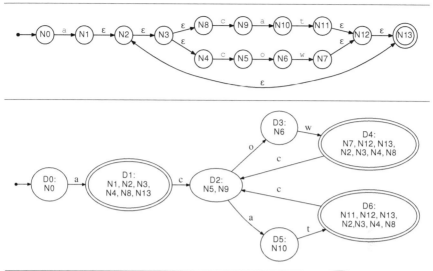

Figure 3.4: Converting an NFA to a DFA via Subset Construction

Example. Let's work out the algorithm on the NFA in Figure 3.4. This is the same NFA corresponding to the RE a(cat | cow) * with each of the states numbered for clarity.

1. Compute D_0 which is ϵ-closure(N_0). N_0 has no ϵ transitions, so $D_0 = \{N_0\}$. Add D_0 to the work list.

2. Remove D_0 from the work list. The character a is an outgoing transition from N_0 to N_1. ϵ-closure(N_1) = $\{N_1, N_2, N_3, N_4, N_8, N_{13}\}$ so add all of those to new state D_1 and add D_1 to the work list.

3. Remove D_1 from the work list. We can see that $N_4 \xrightarrow{c} N_5$ and $N_8 \xrightarrow{c} N_9$, so we create a new state $D_2 = \{N_5, N_9\}$ and add it to the work list.

4. Remove D_2 from the work list. Both a and o are possible transitions because of $N_5 \xrightarrow{o} N_6$ and $N_9 \xrightarrow{a} N_{10}$. So, create a new state D_3 for the o transition to N_6 and new state D_5 for the a transition to N_{10}. Add both D_3 and D_5 to the work list.

5. Remove D_3 from the work list. The only possible transition is $N_6 \xrightarrow{w} N_7$ so create a new state D_4 containing the ϵ-closure(N_7) and add it to the work list.

6. Remove D_5 from the work list. The only possible transition is $N_{10} \xrightarrow{t} N_{11}$ so create a new state D_6 containing ϵ-closure(N_{11}) and add it to the work list.

7. Remove D_4 from the work list, and observe that the only outgoing transition c leads to states N_5 and N_9 which already exist as state D_2, so simply add a transition $D_4 \xrightarrow{c} D_2$.

8. Remove D_6 from the work list and, in a similar way, add $D_6 \xrightarrow{c} D_2$.

9. The work list is empty, so we are done.

3.5.3 Minimizing DFAs

The subset construction algorithm will definitely generate a valid DFA, but the DFA may possibly be very large (especially if we began with a complex NFA generated from an RE.) A large DFA will have a large transition matrix that will consume a lot of memory. If it doesn't fit in L1 cache, the scanner could run very slowly. To address this problem, we can apply Hopcroft's algorithm to shrink a DFA into a smaller (but equivalent) DFA.

The general approach of the algorithm is to optimistically group together all possibly-equivalent states S into super-states T. Initially, we place all non-accepting S states into super-state T_0 and accepting states into super-state T_1. Then, we examine the outgoing edges in each state $s \in T_i$. If, a given character c has edges that begin in T_i and end in *different* super-states, then we consider the super-state to be *inconsistent* with respect to c. (Consider an impermissible transition as if it were a transition to T_E, a super-state for errors.) The super-state must then be split into multiple states that are consistent with respect to c. Repeat this process for all super-states and all characters $c \in \Sigma$ until no more splits are required.

DFA Minimization Algorithm.
Given a DFA with states S, create an equivalent DFA with an equal or fewer number of states T.

First partition S into T such that:
    T_0 = non-accepting states of S.
    T_1 = accepting states of S.
Repeat:
    $\forall T_i \in T$:
        $\forall c \in \Sigma$:
            if $T_i \xrightarrow{c}$ { more than one T state },
            then split T_i into multiple T states
            such that c has the same action in each.
Until no more states are split.

Figure 3.5: Hopcroft's DFA Minimization Algorithm

Example. Suppose we have the following non-optimized DFA and wish to reduce it to a smaller DFA:

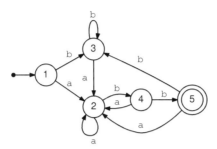

We begin by grouping all of non-accepting states 1, 2, 3, 4 into one super-state and the accepting state 5 into another super-state, like this:

Now, we ask whether this graph is consistent with respect to all possible inputs, by referring back to the original DFA. For example, we observe that, if we are in super-state (1,2,3,4) then an input of a always goes to state 2, which keeps us within the super-state. So, this DFA is consistent with respect to a. However, from super-state (1,2,3,4) an input of b can either stay within the super-state or go to super-state (5). So, the DFA is inconsistent with respect to b.

To fix this, we try splitting out one of the inconsistent states (4) into a new super-state, taking the transitions with it:

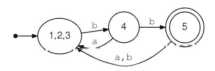

Again, we examine each super-state for consistency with respect to each input character. Again, we observe that super-state 1,2,3 is consistent with respect to a, but not consistent with respect to b because it can either lead to state 3 or state 4. We attempt to fix this by splitting out state 2 into its own super-state, yielding this DFA.

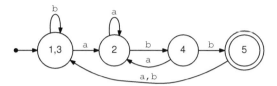

Again, we examine each super-state and observe that each possible input is consistent with respect to the super-state, and therefore we have the minimal DFA.

3.6 Limits of Finite Automata

Regular expressions and finite automata are powerful and effective at recognizing simple patterns in individual words or tokens, but they are not sufficient to analyze all of the structures in a problem. For example, could you use a finite automaton to match an arbitrary number of nested parentheses?

It's not hard to write out an FA that could match, say, up to three pairs of nested parentheses, like this:

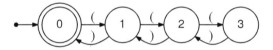

But the key word is *arbitrary*! To match any number of parentheses would require an infinite automaton, which is obviously impractical. Even if we were to apply some practical upper limit (say, 100 pairs) the automaton would still be impractically large when combined with all the other elements of a language that must be supported.

For example, a language like Python permits the nesting of parentheses () for precedence, curly brackets {} to represent object types, and square brackets [] to represent lists. An automaton to match up to 100 nested pairs of each in arbitrary order would have 1,000,000 states!

So, we limit ourselves to using regular expressions and finite automata for the narrow purpose of identifying the words and symbols within a problem. To understand the higher level structure of a program, we will instead use parsing techniques introduced in Chapter 4.

3.7 Using a Scanner Generator

Because a regular expression precisely describes all the allowable forms of a token, we can use a program to automatically transform a set of regular expressions into code for a scanner. Such a program is known as a

```
%{
    (C Preamble Code)
%}

    (Character Classes)
%%

    (Regular Expression Rules)
%%

    (Additional Code)
```

Figure 3.6: Structure of a Flex File

scanner generator. The program Lex, developed at AT&T, was one of the earliest examples of a scanner generator. Vern Paxson translated Lex into the C language to create Flex, which is distributed under the Berkeley license and is widely used in Unix-like operating systems today to generate scanners implemented in C or C++.

To use Flex, we write a specification of the scanner that is a mixture of regular expressions, fragments of C code, and some specialized directives. The Flex program itself consumes the specification and produces regular C code that can then be compiled in the normal way.

Figure 3.6 gives the overall structure of a Flex file. The first section consists of arbitrary C code that will be placed at the beginning of scanner.c, like include files, type definitions, and similar things. Typically, this is used to include a file that contains the symbolic constants for tokens.

The second section states character classes, which are a symbolic shorthand for commonly used regular expressions. For example, you might declare DIGIT [0-9]. This class can be referred to later as {DIGIT}.

The third section is the most important part. It states a regular expression for each type of token that you wish to match, followed by a fragment of C code that will be executed whenever the expression is matched. In the simplest case, this code returns the type of the token, but it can also be used to extract token values, display errors, or anything else appropriate.

The fourth section is arbitrary C code that will go at the end of the scanner, typically for additional helper functions. A peculiar requirement of Flex is that we must define a function yywrap() which returns one to indicate that the input is complete at the end of the file. If we wanted to continue scanning in another file, then yywrap() would open the next file and return zero.

The regular expression language accepted by Flex is very similar to that of formal regular expressions discussed above. The main difference is that characters that have special meaning with a regular expression (like parenthesis, square brackets, and asterisk) must be escaped with a backslash or surrounded with double quotes. Also, a period (.) can be used to match any character at all, which is helpful for catching error conditions.

Contents of File: scanner.flex

```
%{
#include "token.h"
%}
DIGIT   [0-9]
LETTER [a-zA-Z]
%%
(" "|\t|\n)   /* skip whitespace */
\+            { return TOKEN_ADD; }
while         { return TOKEN_WHILE; }
{LETTER}+     { return TOKEN_IDENT; }
{DIGIT}+      { return TOKEN_NUMBER; }
.             { return TOKEN_ERROR; }
%%
int yywrap() { return 1; }
```

Figure 3.7: Example Flex Specification

Contents of File: main.c

```
#include "token.h"
#include <stdio.h>

extern FILE *yyin;
extern int yylex();
extern char *yytext;

int main() {
    yyin = fopen("program.c","r");
    if(!yyin) {
        printf("could not open program.c!\n");
        return 1;
    }

    while(1) {
        token_t t = yylex();
        if(t==TOKEN_EOF) break;
        printf("token: %d  text: %s\n",t,yytext);
    }
}
```

Figure 3.8: Example Main Program

Contents of File: token.h

```
typedef enum {
     TOKEN_EOF=0,
     TOKEN_WHILE,
     TOKEN_ADD,
     TOKEN_IDENT,
     TOKEN_NUMBER,
     TOKEN_ERROR
} token_t;
```

Figure 3.9: Example Token Enumeration

Figure 3.7 shows a simple but complete example to get you started. This specification describes just a few tokens: a single character addition (which must be escaped with a backslash), the `while` keyword, an identifier consisting of one or more letters, and a number consisting of one or more digits. As is typical in a scanner, any other type of character is an error, and returns an explicit token type for that purpose.

Flex generates the scanner code, but not a complete program, so you must write a `main` function to go with it. Figure 3.8 shows a simple driver program that uses this scanner. First, the main program must declare as `extern` the symbols it expects to use in the generated scanner code: `yyin` is the file from which text will be read, `yylex` is the function that implements the scanner, and the array `yytext` contains the actual text of each token discovered.

Finally, we must have a consistent definition of the token types across the parts of the program, so into `token.h` we put an enumeration describing the new type `token_t`. This file is included in both `scanner.flex` and `main.c`.

Figure 3.10 shows how all the pieces come together. `scanner.flex` is converted into `scanner.c` by invoking `flex scanner.flex -o scanner.c`. Then, both `main.c` and `scanner.c` are compiled to produce object files, which are linked together to produce the complete program.

3.8   Practical Considerations

Handling keywords. - In many languages, keywords (such as `while` or `if`) would otherwise match the definitions of identifiers, unless specially handled. There are several solutions to this problem. One is to enter a regular expression for every single keyword into the Flex specification. (These must precede the definition of identifiers, since Flex will accept the first expression that matches.) Another is to maintain a single regular expression that matches all identifiers and keywords. The action associated

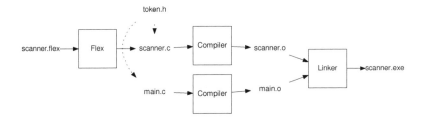

Figure 3.10: Build Procedure for a Flex Program

with that rule can compare the token text with a separate list of keywords and return the appropriate type. Yet another approach is to treat all keywords and identifiers as a single token type, and allow the problem to be sorted out by the parser. (This is necessary in languages like PL/1, where identifiers can have the same names as keywords, and are distinguished by context.)

Tracking source locations. In later stages of the compiler, it is useful for the parser or typechecker to know exactly what line and column number a token was located at, usually to print out a helpful error message. ("Undefined symbol spider at line 153.") This is easily done by having the scanner match newline characters, and increase the line count (but not return a token) each time one is found.

Cleaning tokens. Strings, characters, and similar token types need to be cleaned up after they are matched. For example, `"hello\n"` needs to have its quotes removed and the backslash-n sequence converted to a literal newline character. Internally, the compiler only cares about the actual contents of the string. Typically, this is accomplished by writing a function `string_clean` in the postamble of the Flex specification. The function is invoked by the matching rule before returning the desired token type.

Constraining tokens. Although regular expressions can match tokens of arbitrary length, it does not follow that a compiler must be prepared to accept them. There would be little point to accepting a 1000-letter identifier, or an integer larger than the machine's word size. The typical approach is to set the maximum token length (`YYLMAX` in flex) to a very large value, then examine the token to see if it exceeds a logical limit in the action that matches the token. This allows you to emit an error message that describes the offending token as needed.

Error Handling. The easiest approach to handling errors or invalid input is simply to print a message and exit the program. However, this is unhelpful to users of your compiler – if there are multiple errors, it's (usually) better to see them all at once. A good approach is to match the minimum amount of invalid text (using the dot rule) and return an explicit token type indicating an error. The code that invokes the scanner can then emit a suitable message, and then ask for the next token.

3.9 Exercises

1. Write regular expressions for the following entities. You may find it necessary to justify what is and is not allowed within each expression:

   (a) English days of the week: Monday, Tuesday, ...

   (b) All integers where every three digits are separated by commas for clarity, such as:
   ```
   78
   1,092
   692,098,000
   ```

   (c) Internet email addresses like "John Doe" <john.doe@gmail.com>

   (d) HTTP Uniform Resource Locators (URLs) as described by RFC-1738.

2. Write a regular expression for a string containing any number of X and single pairs of < > and { } which may be nested but not interleaved. For example these strings are allowed:

   ```
   XXX<XX{X}XXX>X
   X{X}X<X>X{X}X<X>X
   ```

   But these are not allowed:

   ```
   XXX<X<XX>>XX
   XX<XX{XX>XX}XX
   ```

3. Test the regular expressions you wrote in the previous two problems by translating them into your favorite programming language that has native support for regular expressions. (Perl and Python are two good choices.) Evaluate the correctness of your program by writing test cases that should (and should not) match.

4. Convert these REs into NFAs using Thompson's construction:

   (a) `for | [a-z]+ | [xb]?[0-9]+`

   (b) `a ( bc*d | ed ) d*`

   (c) `( a*b | b*a | ba )*`

5. Convert the NFAs in the previous problem into DFAs using the subset construction method.

6. Minimize the DFAs in the previous problem by using Hopcroft's algorithm.

7. Write a hand-made scanner for JavaScript Object Notation (JSON) which is described at `http://json.org`. The program should read JSON on the input, and then print out the sequence of tokens observed: LBRACKET, STRING, COLON, etc... Find some large JSON documents online and test your scanner to see if it works.

8. Using Flex, write a scanner for the Java programming language. As above, read in Java source on the input and output token types. Test it out by applying it to a large open source project written in Java.

3.10   Further Reading

1. A.K. Dewdney, "The New Turing Omnibus: Sixty-Six Excursions in Computer Science", Holt Paperbacks, 1992. *An accessible overview of many fundamental problems in computer science – including finite state machines – collected from the author's Mathematical Recreations column in Scientific American.*

2. S. Hollos and J.R. Hollos, "Finite Automata and Regular Expressions: Problems and Solutions", Abrazol Publishing, 2013.
A collection of clever little problems and solutions relating to automata and state machines, if you are looking for more problems to work on.

3. Marvin Minsky, "Computation: Finite and Infinite Machines", Prentice-Hall, 1967.
A classic text offering a more thorough introduction to the theory of finite automata at an undergraduate level.

4. S. Kleene, "Representation of events in nerve nets and finite automata", Automata Studies, C. Shannon and J. McCarthy, editors, Princeton University Press, 1956.

5. R. McNaughton and H. Yamada, "Regular Expressions and State Graphs for Automata", IRE Transactions on Electronic Computers, volume EC-9, number 1, 1960.
http://dx.doi.org/10.1109/TEC.1960.5221603

6. K. Thompson, "Programming Techniques: Regular Expression Search Algorithm", Communications of the ACM, volume 11, number 6, 1968.
http://dx.doi.org/10.1145/363347.363387

Chapter 4 – Parsing

4.1 Overview

If scanning is like constructing words out of letters, then parsing is like constructing sentences out of words in a natural language. Of course, not every sequence of words makes a valid sentence: "horse aircraft conjugate" is three valid words, but not a meaningful sentence.

To parse a computer program, we must first describe the form of valid sentences in a language. This formal statement is known as a context free grammar (CFG). Because they allow for recursion, CFGs are more powerful than regular expressions and can express a richer set of structures.

While a plain CFG is relatively easy to write, it does not follow that is it easy to parse. An arbitrary CFG can contain ambiguities and other problems that make it difficult to write an automatic parser. Therefore, we consider two subsets of CFGs known as LL(1) and LR(1) grammars.

LL(1) grammars are CFGs that can be evaluated by considering only the current rule and next token in the input stream. This property makes it easy to write a hand-coded parser known as a recursive descent parser. However, a language (and its grammar) must be carefully designed (and occasionally rewritten) in order to ensure that it is an LL(1) grammar. Not all language structures can be expressed as LL(1) grammars.

LR(1) grammars are more general and more powerful than LL(1). Nearly all useful programming languages can be written in LR(1) form. However, the parsing algorithm for LR(1) grammars is more complex and usually cannot be written by hand. Instead, it is common to use a parser generator that will accept an LR(1) grammar and automatically generate the parsing code.

4.2 Context Free Grammars

Let's begin by defining the parts of a CFG.

A **terminal** is a discrete symbol that can appear in the language, otherwise known as a token from the previous chapter. Examples of terminals are keywords, operators, and identifiers. We will use lower case letters to represent terminals. At this stage, we only need consider the kind (e.g. integer literal) and not the value (e.g. 456) of a terminal.

A **non-terminal** represents a structure that can occur in a language, but is not a literal symbol. Example of non-terminals are declarations, statements, and expressions. We will use upper-case letters to represent non-terminals: P for program, S for statement, E for expression, etc.

A **sentence** is a valid sequence of terminals in a language, while a **sentential form** is a valid sequence of terminals and non-terminals. We will use Greek symbols to represent sentential forms. For example, α, β, and γ represent (possibly) mixed sequences of terminals and non-terminals.

A **context-free grammar (CFG)** is a list of **rules** that formally describe the allowable sentences in a language. The left-hand side of each rule is always a single non-terminal. The right-hand side of a rule is a sentential form that describes an allowable form of that non-terminal. For example, the rule A $\rightarrow$ xXy indicates that the non-terminal A represents a terminal x followed by a non-terminal X and a terminal y. The right hand side of a rule can be ϵ to indicate that the rule produces nothing. The first rule is special: it is the top-level definition of a program and its non-terminal is known as the **start symbol**.

For example, here is a simple CFG that describes expressions involving addition, integers, and identifiers:

Grammar G$_2$

1. P $\rightarrow$ E
2. E $\rightarrow$ E + E
3. E $\rightarrow$ ident
4. E $\rightarrow$ int

This grammar can be read as follows: (1) A complete program consists of one expression. (2) An expression can be any expression plus any expression. (3) An expression can be an identifier. (4) An expression can be an integer literal.

For brevity, we occasionally condense a set of rules with a common left-hand side by combining all of the right hand sides with a logical-or symbol, like this:

$$E \rightarrow E + E|\text{ident}|\text{int}$$

4.2.1 Deriving Sentences

Each grammar describes a (possibly infinite) set of sentences, which is known as the **language** of the grammar. To prove that a given sentence is a member of that language, we must show that there exists a sequence of rule applications that connects the start symbol with the desired sentence. A sequence of rule applications is known as a **derivation** and a double arrow ($\Rightarrow$) is used to show that one sentential form is equal to another by applying a given rule. For example:

- E $\Rightarrow$ int by applying rule 4 of Grammar G_2

- E + E $\Rightarrow$ E + ident by applying rule 3 of Grammar G_2.

- P $\Rightarrow$ int + ident   by applying all rules of Grammar G_2.

There are two approaches to derivation: top-down and bottom-up.

In **top-down derivation**, we begin with the start symbol, and then apply rules in the CFG to expand non-terminals until reaching the desired sentence. For example, **ident + int + int** is a sentence in this language, and here is one derivation to prove it:

Sentential Form	Apply Rule
P	P $\rightarrow$ E
E	E $\rightarrow$ E + E
E + E	E $\rightarrow$ ident
ident + E	E $\rightarrow$ E + E
ident + E + E	E $\rightarrow$ int
ident + int + E	E $\rightarrow$ int
ident + int + int	

In **bottom-up derivation**, we begin with the desired sentence, and then apply the rules backwards until reaching the start symbol. Here is a bottom-up derivation of the same sentence:

Sentential Form	Apply Rule
ident + int + int	E $\rightarrow$ int
ident + int + E	E $\rightarrow$ int
ident + E + E	E $\rightarrow$ E+E
ident + E	E $\rightarrow$ ident
E + E	E $\rightarrow$ E+E
E	P $\rightarrow$ E
P	

Be careful to distinguish between a *grammar* which is a finite set of rules) and a *language* (which is a set of strings generated by a grammar). It is quite possible for two different grammars to generate the same language, in which case they have **weak equivalence**.

4.2.2 Ambiguous Grammars

An **ambiguous grammar** allows for more than one possible derivation of the same sentence. Our example grammar is ambiguous because there are two possible derivations for any sentence involving two plus signs. The sentence `ident + int + int` can have the two derivations shown in Figure 4.1.

Left-Most Derivation   Right-Most Derivation

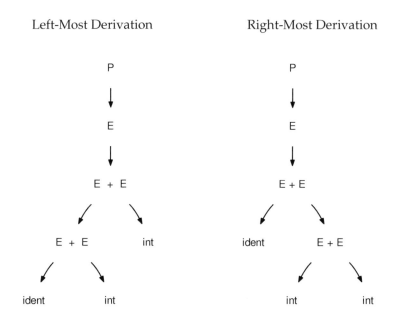

Figure 4.1: Two Derivations of the Same Sentence

Ambiguous grammars present a real problem for parsing (and language design in general) because we do not want a program to have two possible meanings.

Does it matter in this example? It certainly does! In a language like Java, the + operator indicates addition between integers, but concatenation between strings. If the identifier is `hello` and the two integers have the value 5, then the left-most derivation would concatenate all three together into `hello55`, while the right-most derivation would compute 5+5=10 and concatenate the result into `hello10`.

Fortunately, it is usually possible to re-write a grammar so that it is not ambiguous. In the common case of binary operators, we can require that one side of the expression be an atomic term (T), like this:

Grammar G$_3$

1. P $\rightarrow$ E
2. E $\rightarrow$ E + T
3. E $\rightarrow$ T
4. T $\rightarrow$ ident
5. T $\rightarrow$ int

With this change, the grammar is no longer ambiguous, because it only allows a left-most derivation. But also note that it *still accepts the same language as Grammar* G_2. That is any sentence that can be derived by Grammar G_2 can also be derived by Grammar G_3, but there exists only one derivation (and one meaning) per sentence. (Proof is left as an exercise to the reader.)

Now suppose that we would like to add more operators to our grammar. If we simply add more rules of the form $E \rightarrow E * T$ and $E \rightarrow E \div T$, we would still have an unambiguous grammar, but it would not follow the rules of precedence in algebra: each operator would be applied from left to right.

Instead, the usual approach is to construct a grammar with multiple levels that reflect the intended precedence of operators. For example, we can combine addition and multiplication by expressing them as a sum of terms (T) that consist of multiplied factors (F), like this:

Grammar G_4

```
1. P → E
2. E → E + T
3. E → T
4. T → T * F
5. T → F
6. F → ident
7. F → int
```

Here is another common example that occurs in most programming languages in some form or another. Suppose that an `if` statement has two variations: an if-then which takes an action when an expression is true, and an if-then-else that takes a different action for the true and false cases. We can express this fragment of the language like this:

Grammar G_5

```
1. P → S
2. S → if E then S
3. S → if E then S else S
4. S → other
```

Grammar G_5 is ambiguous because it allows for two derivations of this sentence: if E then if E then other else other. Do you see the problem? The `else` part could belong to the outer `if` or to the inner `if`. In most programming languages, the `else` is defined as belonging to the inner `if`, but the grammar does not reflect this.

Do this now:
Write out the two possible parse trees for this sentence:
`if E then if E then other else other.`

4.3   LL Grammars

LL(1) grammars are a subset of CFGs that are easy to parse with simple algorithms. A grammar is LL(1) if it can be parsed by considering only one non-terminal and the next token in the input stream.

To ensure that a grammar is LL(1), we must do the following:

- Remove any ambiguity, as shown above.

- Eliminate any left recursion, as shown below.

- Eliminate any common left prefixes, as shown below.

Once we have taken those steps, then we can prove that it is LL(1) by generating the FIRST and FOLLOW sets for the grammar, and using them to create the LL(1) parse table. If the parse table contains no conflicts, then the grammar is clearly LL(1).

4.3.1   *Eliminating Left Recursion*

LL(1) grammars cannot contain **left recursion**, which is a rule of the form $A \rightarrow A\alpha$ or, more generally, any rule $A \rightarrow B\beta$ such that $B \Rightarrow A\gamma$ by some sequence of derivations. For example, the rule E $\rightarrow$ E + T is left-recursive because E appears as the first symbol on the right hand side.

You might be tempted to solve the problem by simply re-writing the rule as E $\rightarrow$ T + E. While that would avoid left-recursion, it would not be an equivalent grammar because it would result in a right-associative plus operator. Also, it would introduce the new problem of a common left prefix, discussed below.

Informally, we must re-write the rules so that the (formerly) recursive rule begins with the leading symbols of its alternatives.

Formally, if you have a grammar of the form:

$$A \rightarrow A\alpha_1 | A\alpha_2 | ... | \beta_1 | \beta_2 | ...$$

Substitute with:

$$A \rightarrow \beta_1 A' | \beta_2 A' | ...$$

$$A' \rightarrow \alpha_1 A' | \alpha_2 A' | ... | \epsilon$$

Applying this rule to grammar Grammar G_3, we can re-write it as:

Grammar G_6

1. P → E
2. E → T E'
3. E' → + T E'
4. E' → ε
5. T → ident
6. T → int

While Grammar G_6 is perhaps slightly harder for a person to read, it no longer contains left recursion, and satisfies all the LL(1) properties. A parser considering an E in rule 2 will immediately consider the T non-terminal, and then look at ident or int on the input to decide between rule 5 and 6. After considering T, the parser moves on to consider E' and can distinguish between rule 3 and 4 by looking for either a + or any other symbol on the input.

4.3.2 Eliminating Common Left Prefixes

A simpler problem to solve is grammars that have multiple rules with the same left hand side and a common prefix of tokens on the right hand side. Informally, we simply look for all common prefixes of a given non-terminal, and replace them with one rule that contains the prefix, and another that contains the variants.

Formally, look for rules of this form:

$$A \rightarrow \alpha\beta_1 | \alpha\beta_2 | ...$$

And replace with:

$$A \rightarrow \alpha A'$$

$$A' \rightarrow \beta_1 | \beta_2 | ...$$

For example, these rules describing an identifier, array reference, and function call all share the same prefix of a single identifier:

Grammar G_7

1. P → E
2. E → id
3. E → id [E]
4. E → id (E)

If a parser is evaluating E and sees an id on the input, that information is not sufficient to distinguish between rules 2, 3, and 4. However, the grammar can be salvaged by factoring out the common prefix, like this:

Grammar G$_8$

1. P $\rightarrow$ E
2. E $\rightarrow$ id E'
3. E' $\rightarrow$ [E]
4. E' $\rightarrow$ (E)
5. E' $\rightarrow$ ϵ

In this formulation, the parser always consumes an `id` when evaluating an E. If the next token is [, then rule 3 is applied. If the next token is (, then rule 4 is applied, otherwise, rule 5 is applied.

4.3.3   First and Follow Sets

In order to construct a complete parser for an LL(1) grammar, we must compute two sets, known as FIRST and FOLLOW. Informally, FIRST(α) indicates the set of terminals (including ϵ) that could potentially appear at the beginning of any derivation of α. FOLLOW(A) indicates the set of terminals (including $) that could potentially occur after any derivation of the non-terminal A. Given the contents of these sets, an LL(1) parser will always know which rule to pick next.

Here is how to compute FIRST and FOLLOW:

Computing First Sets for a Grammar G

FIRST(α) is the set of terminals that begin all strings given by α, including ϵ if $\alpha \Rightarrow \epsilon$.

For each terminal $a \in \Sigma$: FIRST(a) = $\{a\}$

Repeat:
    For each rule $X \rightarrow Y_1Y_2...Y_k$ in a grammar G:
        Add a to FIRST(X)
            if a is in FIRST(Y_1)
            or a is in FIRST(Y_n) and $Y_1...Y_{n-1} \rightarrow \epsilon$
        If $Y_1...Y_k \rightarrow \epsilon$ then add ϵ to FIRST(X).
until no more changes occur.

Computing Follow Sets for a Grammar G

FOLLOW(A) is the set of terminals that can come after non-terminal A, including $ if A occurs at the end of the input.

FOLLOW(S) = {$} where S is the start symbol.

Repeat:
    If A → $\alpha B \beta$ then:
        add FIRST(β) to FOLLOW(B).
    If A → αB or FIRST(β) contains ϵ then:
        add FOLLOW(A) to FOLLOW(B).
until no more changes occur.

Here is an example of computing FIRST and FOLLOW for Grammar G_9:

Grammar G_9

1. P → E
2. E → T E'
3. E' → + T E'
4. E' → ϵ
5. T → F T'
6. T' → * F T'
7. T' → ϵ
8. F → (E)
9. F → int

First and Follow for Grammar G_9

	P	E	E'	T	T'	F
FIRST	(int	(int	+ ϵ	(int	* ϵ	(int
FOLLOW	$	) $	) $	+) $	+) $	+ *) $

Once we have cleaned up a grammar to be LL(1) and computed its FIRST and FOLLOW sets, we are ready to write code for a parser. This can be done by hand or with a table-driven approach.

4.3.4   Recursive Descent Parsing

LL(1) grammars are very amenable to writing simple hand-coded parsers. A common approach is a **recursive descent parser** in which there is one simple function for each non-terminal in the grammar. The body of the function follows the right-hand sides of the corresponding rules: non-terminals result in a call to another parse function, while terminals result in considering the next token.

Three helper functions are needed:

- `scan_token()` returns the next token on the input stream.

- `putback_token(t)` puts an unexpected token back on the input stream, where it will be read again by the next call to `scan_token`.

- `expect_token(t)` calls `scan_token` to retrieve the next token. It returns true if the token matches the expected type. If not, it puts the token back on the input stream and returns false.

Figure 4.2 shows how Grammar G_9 could be written as a recursive descent parser. Note that the parser has one function for each non-terminal: `parse_P`, `parse_E`, etc. Each function returns true (1) if the input matches the grammar, or false (0) otherwise.

Two special cases should be considered. First, if a rule X cannot produce ϵ and we encounter a token not in $\text{FIRST}(X)$, then we have definitely encountered a parsing error, and we should display a message and return failure. Second, if a rule X *could* produce ϵ and we encounter a token not in $\text{FIRST}(X)$, then we accept the rule $X \to \epsilon$ put the token back on the input, and return success. Another rule will expect to consume that token.

There is also the question of what the parser should actually *do* after matching some element of the grammar. In our simple example, the parser simply returns true on a match, and serves only to verify that the input program matches the grammar. If we wished to actually evaluate the expression, each `parse_X` function could compute the result and return it as a `double`. This would effectively give us a simple interpreter for this language. Another approach is for each `parse_X` function to return a data structure representing that node of the parse tree. As each node is parsed, the result is assembled into an abstract syntax tree, with the root returned by `parse_P`.

```
int parse_P() {
    return parse_E() && expect_token(TOKEN_EOF);
}

int parse_E() {
    return parse_T() && parse_E_prime();
}

int parse_E_prime() {
    token_t t = scan_token();
    if(t==TOKEN_PLUS) {
        return parse_T() && parse_E_prime();
    } else {
        putback_token(t);
        return 1;
    }
}

int parse_T() {
    return parse_F() && parse_T_prime();
}

int parse_T_prime() {
    token_t t = scan_token();
    if(t==TOKEN_MULTIPLY) {
        return parse_F() && parse_T_prime();
    } else {
        putback_token(t);
        return 1;
    }
}

int parse_F() {
    token_t t = scan_token();
    if(t==TOKEN_LPAREN) {
        return parse_E() && expect_token(TOKEN_RPAREN);
    } else if(t==TOKEN_INT) {
        return 1;
    } else {
        printf("parse error: unexpected token %s\n",
            token_string(t));
        return 0;
    }
}
```

Figure 4.2: A Recursive-Descent Parser

4.3.5   Table Driven Parsing

An LL(1) grammar can also be parsed using generalized table driven code. A table-driven parser requires a grammar, a parse table, and a stack to represent the current set of non-terminals.

The **LL(1) parse table** is used to determine which rule should be applied for any combination of non-terminal on the stack and next token on the input stream. (By definition, an LL(1) grammar has exactly one rule to be applied for each combination.) To create a parse table, we use the FIRST and FOLLOW sets like this:

LL(1) Parse Table Construction.
Given a grammar G and alphabet Σ, create a parse table $T[A, a]$ that selects a rule for each combination of non-terminal $A \in G$ and terminal $a \in \Sigma$.

For each rule $A \rightarrow \alpha$ in G:
    For each terminal a (excepting ϵ) in FIRST(α):
        Add $A \rightarrow \alpha$ to $T[A, a]$.
    If ϵ is in FIRST(α):
        For each terminal b (including $) in FOLLOW($A$):
            Add A $\rightarrow \alpha$ to $T[A, b]$.

For example, here is the parse table for Grammar G_9. Notice that the entries for P, E, T, and F are straightforward: each can only start with int or (, and so these tokens cause the rules to descend toward F and a choice between rule 8 ($F \rightarrow int$) and rule 9 ($F \rightarrow (E)$). The entry for E' is a little more complicated: a + token results in applying $E \rightarrow +TE'$, while) or $ indicates $E \rightarrow \epsilon$.

Parse Table for Grammar G_9:

	int	+	*	(	)	$
P	1			1		
E	2			2		
E'		3			4	4
T	5			5		
T'		7	6		7	7
F	9			8		

Now we have all the pieces necessary to operate the parser. Informally, the idea is to keep a stack which tracks the current state of the parser. In each step, we consider the top element of the stack and the next token on the input. If they match, then pop the stack, accept the token and continue. If not, then consult the parse table for the next rule to apply. If we can continue until the end-of-file symbol is matched, then the parse succeeds.

LL(1) Table Parsing Algorithm.
Given a grammar G with start symbol P and parse table T, parse a sequence of tokens and determine whether they satisfy G.

Create a stack S.
Push $ and P onto S.
Let c be the first token on the input.

While S is not empty:
    Let X be the top element of the stack.
    If X matches c:
        Remove X from the stack.
        Advance c to the next token and repeat.
    If X is any other terminal, stop with an error.
    If $T[X, c]$ indicates rule $X \to \alpha$:
        Remove X from the stack.
        Push symbols α on to the stack and repeat.
    If $T[X, c]$ indicates an error state, stop with an error.

Here is an example of the algorithm applied to the sentence `int * int`:

Stack	Input	Action
P $	int * int $	apply 1: P $\Rightarrow$ E
E $	int * int $	apply 2: E $\Rightarrow$ T E'
T E' $	int * int $	apply 5: T $\Rightarrow$ F T'
F T' E' $	int * int $	apply 9: F $\Rightarrow$ int
int T' E' $	* int $	match int
T' E' $	* int $	apply 6: T' $\Rightarrow$ * F T'
* F T' E' $	* int $	match *
F T' E' $	int $	apply 9: F $\Rightarrow$ int
int T' E' $	int $	match int
T' E' $	$	apply 7: T' $\Rightarrow$ ϵ
E' $	$	apply 4: E' $\Rightarrow$ ϵ
$	$	match $

4.4   LR Grammars

While LL(1) grammars and top-down parsing techniques are easy to work with, they are not able to represent all of the structures found in many programming languages. For more general-purpose programming languages, we must use an LR(1) grammar and associated bottom-up parsing techniques.

LR(1) is the set of grammars that can be parsed via shift-reduce techniques with a single character of lookahead. LR(1) is a super-set of LL(1) and can accommodate left recursion and common left prefixes which are not permitted in LL(1). This enables us to express many programming constructs in a more natural way. (An LR(1) grammar must still be non-ambiguous, and it cannot have shift-reduce or reduce-reduce conflicts, which we will explain below.)

For example, Grammar G_{10} is an LR(1) grammar:

Grammar G_{10}

1. P $\rightarrow$ E
2. E $\rightarrow$ E + T
3. E $\rightarrow$ T
4. T $\rightarrow$ id (E)
5. T $\rightarrow$ id

We need to know the FIRST and FOLLOW sets of LR(1) grammars as well, so take a moment now and work out the sets for Grammar G_{10}, using the same technique from section 4.3.3.

	P	E	T
FIRST			
FOLLOW			

4.4.1 Shift-Reduce Parsing

LR(1) grammars must be parsed using the **shift-reduce** parsing technique. This is a bottom-up parsing strategy that begins with the tokens and looks for rules that can be applied to reduce sentential forms into non-terminals. If there is a sequence of reductions that leads to the start symbol, then the parse is successful.

A **shift** action consumes one token from the input stream and pushes it onto the stack. A **reduce** action applies one rule of the form $A \rightarrow \alpha$ from the grammar, replacing the sentential form α on the stack with the non-terminal A. For example, here is a shift-reduce parse of the sentence `id(id+id)` using Grammar G_{10}:

Stack	Input	Action
	id (id + id) $	shift
id	(id + id) $	shift
id (	id + id) $	shift
id (id	+ id) $	reduce T → id
id (T	+ id) $	reduce T → E
id (E	+ id) $	shift
id (E +	id) $	shift
id (E + id	) $	reduce T → id
id (E + T	) $	reduce E → E + T
id (E	) $	shift
id (E)	$	reduce T → id(E)
T	$	reduce E → T
E	$	reduce E → P
P	$	accept

While this example shows that there exists a derivation for the sentence, it does not explain how each action was chosen at each step. For example, in the second step, we might have chosen to reduce `id` to T instead of shifting a left parenthesis. This would have been a bad choice, because there is no rule that begins with T (, but that was not immediately obvious without attempting to proceed further. To make these decisions, we must analyze LR(1) grammars in more detail.

4.4.2   The LR(0) Automaton

An **LR(0) automaton** represents all the possible rules that are currently under consideration by a shift-reduce parser. (The LR(0) automaton is also variously known as the **canonical collection** or the **compact finite state machine** of the grammar.) Figure 4.6 shows a complete automaton for Grammar G_{10}. Each box represents a state in the machine, connected by transitions for both terminals and non-terminals in the grammar.

Each state in the automaton consists of multiple **items**, which are rules augmented by a **dot** (.) that indicates the parser's current position in that rule. For example, the configuration $E \rightarrow E . + T$ indicates that E is currently on the stack, and $+$ T is a possible next sequence of tokens.

The automaton is constructed as follows. State 0 is created taking the production for the start symbol ($P \rightarrow E$) and adding a dot at the beginning of the right hand side. This indicates that we expect to see a complete program, but have not yet consumed any symbols. This is known as the **kernel** of the state.

Kernel of State 0

$$\boxed{P \rightarrow . E}$$

Then, we compute the **closure** of the state as follows. For each item in the state with a non-terminal X immediately to the right of the dot, we add all rules in the grammar that have X as the left hand side. The newly added items have a dot at the beginning of the right hand side.

$$\boxed{\begin{array}{l} P \rightarrow . E \\ E \rightarrow . E + T \\ E \rightarrow . T \end{array}}$$

The procedure continues until no new items can be added:

Closure of State 0

$$\boxed{\begin{array}{l} P \rightarrow . E \\ E \rightarrow . E + T \\ E \rightarrow . T \\ T \rightarrow . id (E) \\ T \rightarrow . id \end{array}}$$

You can think of the state this way: It describes the initial state of the parser as expecting a complete program in the form of an E. However, an E is known to begin with an E or a T, and a T must begin with an id. All of those symbols could represent the beginning of the program.

From this state, all of the symbols (terminals and non-terminals both) to the right of the dot are possible outgoing transitions. If the automaton takes that transition, it moves to a new state containing the matching items, with the dot moved one position to the right. The closure of the new state is computed, possibly adding new rules as described above.

For example, from state zero, E, T, and id are the possible transitions, because each appears to the right of the dot in some rule. Here are the states for each of those transitions:

Transition on E:

$P \rightarrow E$.
$E \rightarrow E$. $+ T$

Transition on T:

$E \rightarrow T$.

Transition on id:

$T \rightarrow id$. (E)
$T \rightarrow id$.

Figure 4.3 gives the complete LR(0) automaton for Grammar G_{10}. Take a moment now to trace over the table and be sure that you understand how it is constructed.

No, really. Stop now and study the figure carefully before continuing.

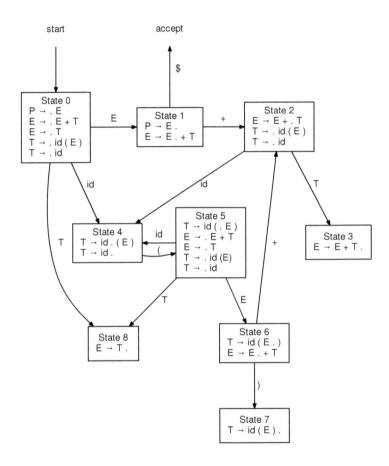

Figure 4.3: LR(0) Automaton for Grammar G_{10}

The LR(0) automaton tells us the choices available at any step of bottom up parsing. When we reach a state containing an item with a dot at the end of the rule, that indicates a possible reduction. A transition on a terminal that moves the dot one position to the right indicates a possible shift. While the LR(0) automaton tells us the available actions at each step, it does not always tell us *which* action to take.[1]

Two types of conflicts can appear in an LR grammar:

A **shift-reduce conflict** indicates a choice between a shift action and a reduce action. For example, state 4 offers a choice between shifting a left parenthesis and reducing by rule five:

$$
\text{Shift-Reduce Conflict:} \quad
\begin{array}{|l|}
\hline
T \rightarrow \text{id} . (E) \\
T \rightarrow \text{id} . \\
\hline
\end{array}
$$

A **reduce-reduce conflict** indicates that two distinct rules have been completely matched, and either one could apply. While Grammar G_{10} does not contain any reduce-reduce conflicts, they commonly occur when a syntactic structure occurs at multiple layers in a grammar. For example, it is often the case that a function invocation can be a statement by itself, or an element within an expression. The automaton for such a grammar would contain a state like this:

$$
\text{Reduce-Reduce Conflict:} \quad
\begin{array}{|l|}
\hline
S \rightarrow \text{id} (E) . \\
E \rightarrow \text{id} (E) . \\
\hline
\end{array}
$$

The LR(0) automaton forms the basis of LR parsing, by telling us which actions are available in each state. But, it does not tell us *which* action to take or how to resolve shift-reduce and reduce-reduce conflicts. To do that, we must take into account some additional information.

---

[1] The 0 in LR(0) indicates that it uses zero lookahead tokens, which is a way of saying that it does not consider the input before making a decision. While it is possible to write out a grammar that is strictly LR(0), it is not very interesting or useful, since the parse does not depend on the input!

4.4.3   SLR Parsing

Simple LR (SLR) parsing is a basic form of LR parsing in which we use
FOLLOW sets to resolve conflicts in the LR(0) automaton. In short, we
take the reduction A → α only when the next token on the input is in
FOLLOW(A). If a grammar can be parsed by this technique, we say it is an
SLR grammar, which is a subset of LR(1) grammars.

For example, the shift-reduce conflict in state 4 of Figure 4.6 is resolved
by consulting FOLLOW(T). If the next token is +,) or $, then we reduce
by rule T → id. If the next token is (, then we shift to state 5. If neither of
those is true, then the input is invalid, and we emit a parse error.

These decisions are encoded in the **SLR parse tables** which are known
historically as GOTO and ACTION. The tables are created as follows:

SLR Parse Table Creation.

Given a grammar G and corresponding LR(0) automaton,
create tables ACTION[s, a] and GOTO[s, A] for all states s,
terminals a, and non-terminals A in G.

For each state s:
    For each item like A → α . a β
        ACTION[s, a] = **shift** to state t according to the LR(0) automaton.
    For each item like A → α . B β
        GOTO[s, B] = **goto** state t according to the LR(0) automaton.
    For each item like A → α .
        For each terminal a in FOLLOW(A):
            ACTION[s, a] = **reduce** by rule A → α

All remaining states are considered error states.

Naturally, each state in the table can be occupied by only one action.
If following the procedure results in a table with more than one state in a
given entry, then you can conclude that the grammar is not SLR. (It might
still be LR(1) – more on that below.)

Here is the SLR parse table for Grammar G_{10}. Note carefully the states 1 and 4 where there is a choice between shifting and reducing. In state 1, a lookahead of + causes a shift, while a lookahead of $ results in a reduction $P \to E$ because $ is the only member of FOLLOW(P).

State	GOTO		ACTION				
	E	T	id	(	)	+	$
0	G1	G8	S4				
1						S2	R1
2		G3	S4				
3					R2	R2	R2
4				S5	R5	R5	R5
5	G6	G8	S4				
6						S7	S2
7					R4	R4	R4
8					R3	R3	R3

Figure 4.4: SLR Parse Table for Grammar G_{10}

Now we are ready to parse an input by following the SLR parsing algorithm. The parse requires maintaining a stack of states in the LR(0) automaton, initially containing the start state S_0. Then, we examine the top of the stack and the lookahead token, and take the action indicated by the SLR parse table. On a shift, we consume the token and push the indicated state on the stack. On a reduce by $A \rightarrow \beta$, we pop states from stack corresponding to each of the symbols in β, then take the additional step of moving to state $\text{GOTO}[t, A]$. This process continues until we either succeed by reducing the start symbol, or fail by encountering an error state.

SLR Parsing Algorithm.

Let S be a stack of LR(0) automaton states. Push S_0 onto S.
Let a be the first input token.

Loop:
    Let s be the top of the stack.
    If $\text{ACTION}[s, a]$ is **accept**:
        Parse complete.
    Else if $\text{ACTION}[s, a]$ is **shift** t:
        Push state t on the stack.
        Let a be the next input token.
    Else if $\text{ACTION}[s, a]$ is **reduce** $A \rightarrow \beta$:
        Pop states corresponding to β from the stack.
        Let t be the top of stack
        Push $\text{GOTO}[t, A]$ onto the stack.
    Otherwise:
        Halt with a parse error.

Here is an example of applying the SLR parsing algorithm to the program id (id + id). The first three steps are easy: a shift is performed for each of the first three tokens id (id. The fourth step reduces T → id. This causes state 4 (corresponding to the right hand side id) to be popped from the stack. State 5 is now at the top of the stack, and GOTO[5, T] = 8, so state 8 is pushed, resulting in a stack of 0 4 5 8.

Stack	Symbols	Input	Action
0		id (id + id) $	shift 4
0 4	id	(id + id) $	shift 5
0 4 5	id (	id + id) $	shift 4
0 4 5 4	id (id	+ id) $	reduce T → id
0 4 5 8	id (T	+ id) $	reduce E → T
0 4 5 6	id (E	+ id) $	shift 2
0 4 5 6 2	id (E +	id) $	shift 4
0 4 5 6 2 4	id (E + id	) $	reduce T → id
0 4 5 6 2 3	id (E + T	) $	reduce E → E + T
0 4 5 6	id (E	) $	shift 7
0 4 5 6 7	id (E)	$	reduce T → id(E)
0 8	T	$	reduce E → T
0 1	E	$	accept

(Although we show two columns for "Stack" and "Symbols", they are simply two representations of the same information. The stack state 0 4 5 8 represents the parse state of id (T and vice versa.)

It should now be clear that SLR parsing has the same algorithmic complexity as LL(1) parsing. Both techniques require a parsing table and a stack. At each step in both algorithms, it is necessary to only consider the current state and the next token on the input. The distinction is that each LL(1) parsing state considers only a single non-terminal, while each LR(1) parsing state considers a large number of possible configurations.

SLR parsing is a good starting point for understanding the general principles of bottom up parsing. However, SLR is a subset of LR(1), and not all LR(1) grammars are SLR. For example, consider Grammar G_{11} which allows for a statement to be a variable assignment, or an identifier by itself. Note that FOLLOW(S) = {\$}and FOLLOW(V) = {=|\$}.

Grammar G_{11}

1. S → V = E
2. S → id
3. V → id
4. V → id [E]
5. E → V

We need only build part of the LR(0) automaton to see the problem:

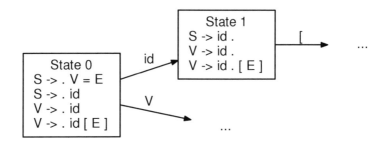

Figure 4.5: Part of LR(0) Automaton for Grammar G_{11}

In state 1, we can reduce by S → id or V → id. However, both FOLLOW(S) and FOLLOW(V) contain \$, so we cannot decide which to take when the next token is end-of-file. Even using the FOLLOW sets, there is still a reduce-reduce conflict. Therefore, Grammar G_{11} is not an SLR grammar.

But, if we look more closely at the possible sentences allowed by the grammar, the distinction between the two becomes clear. Rule S → id would only be applied in the case where the complete sentence is id \$. If any other character follows a leading id, then V → id applies. So, the grammar is not inherently ambiguous: we just need a more powerful parsing algorithm.

4.4.4 LR(1) Parsing

The LR(0) automaton is limited in power, because it does not track what tokens can actually follow a production. SLR parsing accommodates for this weakness by using FOLLOW sets to decide when to reduce. As shown above, this is not sufficiently discriminating to parse all valid LR(1) grammars.

Now we give the complete or "canonical" form of LR(1) parsing, which depends upon the LR(1) automaton. The LR(1) automaton is like the LR(0) automaton, except that each item is annotated with the set of tokens that could potentially follow it, given the current parsing state. This set is known as the **lookahead** of the item. The lookahead is always a subset of the FOLLOW of the relevant non-terminal.

The lookahead of the kernel of the start state is always $\{\$\}$. When computing the closure of an item $A \to \alpha.B\beta$ the newly added rule $B \to .\gamma$ gets a lookahead of $\text{FIRST}(\beta)$.

Here is an example for Grammar G_{11}. The kernel of the start state consists of the start symbol with a lookahead of $\$$:

Kernel of State 0

```
S → . V = E {$}
S → . id      {$}
```

The closure of the start state is computed by adding the rules for V with a lookahead of $=$, because $=$ follows V in rule 1:

Closure of State 0

```
S → . V = E  {$}
S → . id     {$}
V → . id     {=}
V → . id [ E ] {=}
```

Now suppose that we construct state 1 via a transition on the terminal id. The lookahead for each item is propagated to the new state:

Closure of State 1

```
S → id .      {$}
V → id .      {=}
V → id . [ E ] {=}
```

Now you can see how the lookahead solves the reduce-reduce conflict. When the next token on the input is $\$$, we can only reduce by $S \to \text{id}$. When the next token is $=$, we can only reduce by $V \to \text{id}$. By tracking lookaheads in a more fine-grained manner than SLR, we are able to parse arbitrary LR(1) grammars.

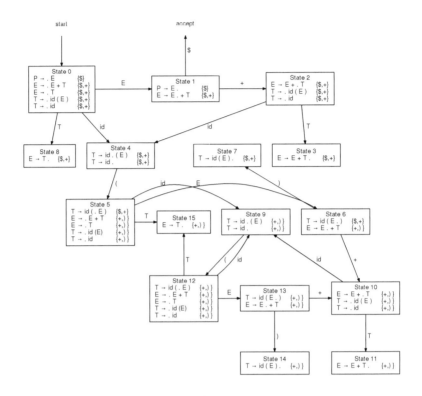

Figure 4.6: LR(1) Automaton for Grammar G_{10}

Figure 4.6 gives the complete LR(1) automaton for Grammar G_{10}. Take a moment now to trace over the table and be sure that you understand how it is constructed.

One aspect of state zero is worth clarifying. When constructing the closure of a state, we must consider *all* rules in the grammar, including the rule corresponding to the item under closure. The item E $\rightarrow$. E + T is initially added with a lookahead of $\{\$\}$. Then, evaluating that item, we add all rules that have E on the left hand side, adding a lookahead of $\{+\}$. So, we add E $\rightarrow$. E + T *again*, this time with a lookahead of $\{+\}$, resulting in a single item with a lookahead set of $\{\$, +\}$

4.4.5 LALR Parsing

The main downside to LR(1) parsing is that the LR(1) automaton can be *much* larger than the LR(0) automaton. Any two states that have the same items but differ in lookahead sets for *any* items are considered to be different states. The result is enormous parse tables that consume large amounts of memory and slow down the parsing algorithm.

Lookahead LR (LALR) parsing is the practical answer to this problem. To construct an LALR parser, we first create the LR(1) automaton, and then merge states that have the same core. The **core** of a state is simply the body of an item, ignoring the lookahead. When several LR(1) items are merged into one LALR item, the LALR lookahead is the union of the lookaheads of the LR(1) items.

For example, these two LR(1) states:

```
E → . E + T {$+}      E → . E + T {)+}
E → . T     {$+}      E → . T     {)+}
```

Would be merged into this single LALR state:

```
E → . E + T {$)+}
E → . T     {$)+}
```

The resulting LALR automaton has the same number of states as the LR(0) automaton, but has more precise lookahead information available for each item. While this may seem a minor distinction, experience has shown this simple improvement to be highly effective at obtaining the efficiency of SLR parsing while accommodating a large number of practical grammars.

4.5 Grammar Classes Revisited

Now that you have some experience working with different kinds of grammars, let's step back and review how they relate to each other.

$$LL(1) \subset SLR \subset LALR \subset LR(1) \subset CFG \tag{4.1}$$

CFG: A context-free grammar is any grammar whose rules have the form $A \rightarrow \alpha$. To parse any CFG, we require a finite automaton (a parse table) and a stack to keep track of the parse state. An arbitrary CFG can be ambiguous. An ambiguous CFG will result in a non-deterministic finite automaton, which is not practical to use. Instead, it is more desirable to re-write the grammar to fit a more restricted class.

LR(k): An LR(k) parser performs a bottom-up **L**eft to right scan of the input and provides a **R**ight-most parse, deciding what rule to apply next by examining the next k tokens on the input. A canonical LR(1) parser requires a very large finite automaton, because the possible lookaheads are encoded into the states. While strictly a subset of CFGs, nearly all real-world language constructs can be expressed adequately in LR(1).

LALR: A Lookahead-LR parser is created by first constructing a canonical LR(1) parser, and then merging all itemsets that have the same core. This yields a much smaller finite automaton, while retaining some detailed lookahead information. While less powerful than canonical LR(1) in theory, LALR is usually sufficient to express real-world languages.

SLR: A Simple-LR parser approximates an LR(1) parser by constructing the LR(0) state machine, and then relying on the FIRST and FOLLOW sets to select which rule to apply. SLR is simple and compact, but there are easy-to-find examples of common constructs that it cannot parse.

LL(k): An LL(k) parser performs a top-down **L**eft to right scan of the input and provides a **L**eft-most parse, deciding what rule to apply next by examining the next k tokens on the input. LL(1) parsers are simple and widely used because they require a table that is only $O(nt)$ where t is the number of tokens, and n is the number of non-terminals. $LL(k)$ parsers are less practical for $k > 1$ because the size of the parse table is $O(nt^k)$ in the worst case.[2] However, they often require that a grammar be rewritten to be more amenable to the parser, and are not able to express all common language structures.

4.6   The Chomsky Hierarchy

Finally, this brings us to a fundamental result in theoretical computer science, known as the **Chomsky hierarchy** [1], named after noted linguist Noam Chomsky. The hierarchy describes four categories of languages (and corresponding grammars) and relates them to the abstract computing machinery necessary to recognize such a language.

Regular languages are those described by regular expressions, as you learned back in Chapter 3. Every regular expression corresponds to a finite automaton that can be used to identify all words in the corresponding language. As you know, a finite automaton can be implemented with the very simple mechanism of a table and a single integer to represent the current state. So, a scanner for a regular language is very easy to implement efficiently.

Context free languages are those described by context free grammars where each rule is of the form A $\rightarrow$ γ, with a single non-terminal on the

---

[2]For example, an LL(1) parser would require a row for terminals $\{a, b, c, \ldots\}$, while an LL(2) parser would require a row for pairs $\{aa, ab, ac, \ldots\}$.

Language Class	Machine Required
Regular Languages	Finite Automata
Context Free Languages	Pushdown Automata
Context Sensitive Languages	Linear Bounded Automata
Recursively Enumerable Languages	Turing Machine

Figure 4.7: The Chomsky Hierarchy

left hand side, and a mix of terminals and non-terminals on the right hand side. We call these "context free" because the meaning of a non-terminal is the same in all places where it appears. As you have learned in this chapter, a CFG requires a pushdown automaton, which is achieved by coupling a finite automaton with a stack. If the grammar is ambiguous, the automaton will be non-deterministic and therefore impractical. In practice, we restrict ourselves to using subsets of CFGs (like LL(1) and LR(1) that are non-ambiguous and result in a deterministic automaton that completes in bounded time.

Context sensitive languages are those described by context sensitive grammars where each rule can be of the form $\alpha A \beta \rightarrow \alpha \gamma \beta$. We call these "context sensitive" because the interpretation of a non-terminal is controlled by context in which it appears. Context sensitive languages require a non-deterministic linear bounded automaton, which is bounded in memory consumption, but not in execution time. Context sensitive languages are not very practical for computer languages.

Recursively enumerable languages are the least restrictive set of languages, described by rules of the form $\alpha \rightarrow \beta$ where α and β can be any combination of terminals and non-terminals. These languages can only be recognized by a full Turing machine, and are the least practical of all.

The Chomsky Hierarchy is a specific example of a more general principle for the design of languages and compilers:

The least powerful language gives the strongest guarantees.

That is to say, if we have a problem to be solved, it should be attacked using the least expressive tool that is capable of addressing the problem. If we *can* solve a given problem by employing REs instead of CFGs, then we *should* use REs, because they consume less state, have simpler machinery, and present fewer roadblocks to a solution.

The same advice applies more broadly: assembly language is the most powerful language available in our toolbox and is capable of expressing any program that the computer is capable of executing. However, assembly language is also the most difficult to use because it gives none of the guarantees found in higher level languages. Higher level languages are *less* powerful than assembly language, and this is what makes them more predictable, reliable, and congenial to use.

4.7   Exercises

1. Write out an improvement to Grammar G_5 that does not have the dangling-else problem. Hint: Prevent the inner S from containing an `if` without an `else`.

2. Write a grammar for an interesting subset of sentences in English, including nouns, verbs, adjectives, adverbs, conjunctions, subordinate phrases, and so forth. (Include just a few terminals in each category to give the idea.) Is the grammar LL(1), LR(1), or ambiguous? Explain why.

3. Consider the following grammar:

Grammar G_{12}

```
 1.  P → S
 2.  P → S P
 3.  S → if E then S
 4.  S → if E then S else S
 5.  S → while E S
 6.  S → begin P end
 7.  S → print E
 8.  S → E
 9.  E → id
10.  E → integer
11.  E → E + E
```

   (a) Point out all aspects of Grammar G_{12} which are not LL(1).

   (b) Write a new grammar which accepts the same language, but avoids left recursion and common left prefixes.

   (c) Write the FIRST and FOLLOW sets for the new grammar.

   (d) Write out the LL(1) parse table for the new grammar.

   (e) Is the new grammar an LL(1) grammar? Explain your answer carefully.

4. Consider the following grammar:

Grammar G_{13}

```
1. S → id = E
2. E → E + P
3. E → P
4. P → id
5. P → (E)
6. P → id(E)
```

    (a) Draw the LR(0) automaton for Grammar G_{13}.

    (b) Write out the complete SLR parsing table for Grammar G_{13}.

    (c) Is this grammar LL(1)? Explain why.

    (d) Is this grammar SLR(1)? Explain why.

5. Consider Grammar G_{11}, shown earlier.

    (a) Write out the complete LR(1) automaton for Grammar G_{11}.

    (b) Compact the LR(1) automaton into the LALR automaton for Grammar G_{11}

6. Write a context free grammar that describes formal regular expressions. Start by writing out the simplest (possibly ambiguous) grammar you can think of, based on the inductive definition in Chapter 3. Then, rewrite the grammar into an equivalent LL(1) grammar.

7. (a) Write a grammar for the JSON data representation language.

    (b) Write the FIRST and FOLLOW sets for your grammar.

    (c) Is your grammar LL(1), SLR, or LR(1), or neither? If necessary, re-write it until it is in the simplest grammar class possible.

    (d) Write out the appropriate parse table for your grammar.

8. Write a working hand-coded parser for JSON expressions, making use of the JSON scanner constructed in the previous chapter.

9. Create a hand-coded scanner and a recursive descent parser that can evaluate first order logic expressions entered on the console. Include boolean values (T/F) and the operators & (and), | (or), ! (not), -> (implication), and () (grouping).

For example, these expressions should evaluate to true:

```
T
T & T | F
( F -> F ) -> T
```

And these expressions should evaluate to false:

```
F
! ( T | F )
( T -> F ) & T
```

10. Write a hand-coded parser that reads in regular expressions and outputs the corresponding NFA, using the Graphviz [2] DOT language.

11. Write a parser-construction tool that reads in an LL(1) grammar and produces working code for a table-driven parser as output.

4.8   Further Reading

1. N. Chomsky, "On certain formal properties of grammars", Information and Control, volume 2, number 2, 1959.
   http://dx.doi.org/10.1016/S0019-9958(59)90362-6

2. J. Ellson, E. Gansner, L. Koutsofios, S. North, G. Woodhull, "Graphviz – Open Source Graph Drawing Tools", International Symposium on Graph Drawing, 2001.
   http://www.graphviz.org

3. J. Earley, "An Efficient Context Free Parsing Algorithm", Communications of the ACM, volume 13, issue 2, 1970.
   https://doi.org/10.1145/362007.362035

4. M. Tomita (editor), "Generalized LR Parsing", Springer, 1991.

Chapter 5 – Parsing in Practice

In this chapter, you will apply what you have learned about the theory of LL(1) and LR(1) grammars in order to build a working parser for a simple expression language. This will give you a basis to write a more complete parser for B-Minor in the following chapter.

While LL(1) parsers are commonly written by hand, LR(1) parsers are simply too cumbersome to do the same. Instead, we rely upon a **parser generator** to take a specification of a grammar and automatically produce the working code. In this chapter, we will give examples with Bison, a widely-used parser generator for C like languages.

Using Bison, we will define an LALR grammar for algebraic expressions, and then employ it to create three different varieties of programs.

- A **validator** reads the input program and then simply informs the user whether it is a valid sentence in the language specified by the grammar. Such a tool is often used to determine whether a given program conforms to one standard or another.

- An **interpreter** reads the input program and then actually executes the program to produce a result. One approach to interpretation is to compute the result of each operation as soon as it is parsed. The alternate approach is to parse the program into an abstract syntax tree, and then execute it.

- A **translator** reads the input program, parses it into an abstract syntax tree, and then traverses the abstract syntax tree to produce an equivalent program in a different format.

5.1   The Bison Parser Generator

It is not practical to implement an LALR parser by hand, and so we rely on tools to automatically generate tables and code from a grammar specification. YACC (Yet Another Compiler Compiler) was a widely used parser generator in the Unix environment, recently supplanted by the GNU Bison parser which is generally compatible. Bison is designed to automatically invoke Flex as needed, so it is easy to combine the two into a complete program.

Just as with the scanner, we must create a specification of the grammar to be parsed, where each rule is accompanied by an action to follow. The overall structure of a Bison file is similar to that of Flex:

```
%{
    (C preamble code)
%}
    (declarations)
%%
    (grammar rules)
%%
    (C postamble code)
```

The first section contains arbitrary C code, typically #include statements and global declarations. The second section can contain a variety of declarations specific to the Bison language. We will use the %token keyword to declare all of the terminals in our language. The main body of the file contains a series of rules of the form

```
expr : expr TOKEN_ADD expr
     | TOKEN_INT
     ;
```

indicating that non-terminal expr can produce the sentence expr TOKEN ADD expr or the single terminal TOKEN_INT. White space is not significant, so it's ok to arrange the rules for clarity. Note that the usual naming convention is reversed: since upper case is customarily used for C constants, we use lower case to indicate non-terminals.

The resulting code creates a single function yyparse() that returns an integer: zero indicates a successful parse, one indicates a parse error, and two indicates an internal problem such as memory exhaustion. yyparse assumes that there exists a function yylex that returns integer token types. This can be written by hand or generated automatically by Flex. In the latter case, the input source can be changed by modifying the file pointer yyin.

Figure 5.1 gives a Bison specification for simple algebraic expressions on integers. Remember that Bison accepts an LR(1) grammar, so it is ok to have left-recursion within the various rules.

```
%{
#include <stdio.h>
%}

%token TOKEN_INT
%token TOKEN_PLUS
%token TOKEN_MINUS
%token TOKEN_MUL
%token TOKEN_DIV
%token TOKEN_LPAREN
%token TOKEN_RPAREN
%token TOKEN_SEMI
%token TOKEN_ERROR

%%
program : expr TOKEN_SEMI;

expr : expr TOKEN_PLUS term
     | expr TOKEN_MINUS term
     | term
     ;

term : term TOKEN_MUL factor
     | term TOKEN_DIV factor
     | factor
     ;

factor: TOKEN_MINUS factor
      | TOKEN_LPAREN expr TOKEN_RPAREN
      | TOKEN_INT
      ;
%%

int yywrap() { return 0; }
```

Figure 5.1: Bison Specification for Expression Validator

```c
#include <stdio.h>

extern int yyparse();

int main()
{
    if(yyparse()==0) {
        printf("Parse successful!\n");
    } else {
        printf("Parse failed.\n");
    }
}
```

Figure 5.2: Main Program for Expression Validator

Figure 5.3 shows the general build procedure for a combined program that uses Bison and Flex together. The parser specification goes in `parser.bison`. We assume that you have written a suitable scanner and placed it in `scanner.flex`. Previously, we wrote `token.h` by hand. Here, we will rely on Bison to generate `token.h` automatically from the `%token` declarations, so that the parser and the scanner are working from the same information. Invoke Bison like this:

```
bison --defines=token.h --output=parser.c parser.bison
```

The `--output=parser.c` option directs Bison to write its code into the file `parser.c` instead of the cryptic `yy.tab.c`. Then, we compile `parser.c`, the `scanner.c` generated by Flex, and `main.c` independently, and link them together into a complete executable.

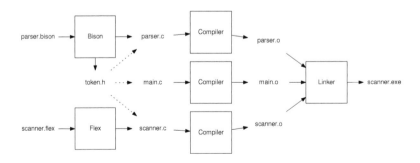

Figure 5.3: Build Procedure for Bison and Flex Together

If you give Bison the −v option, it will output a text representation of the LALR automaton to the file `parser.output`. For each state, it gives the items, using dot to indicate the parser position. Then, it lists the actions applied to that state. For example, suppose that we modify the grammar above so that it becomes ambiguous:

```
expr : expr TOKEN_PLUS expr
```

Bison will report that the grammar has one shift-reduce conflict, and `parser.output` will describe each state. In the event of a conflict, Bison will suppress one or more actions, and this is indicated by square brackets in the following report:

```
state 9
    2 expr: expr . TOKEN_PLUS expr
    2      | expr TOKEN_PLUS expr .

    TOKEN_PLUS  shift, and go to state 7
    TOKEN_PLUS  [reduce using rule 2 (expr)]
    $default    reduce using rule 2 (expr)
```

Be careful! If your grammar has shift-reduce or reduce-reduce conflicts, Bison will happily output working code with some of the conflicting actions suppressed. The code may appear to work on simple inputs, but is likely to have unexpected effects on complete programs. Always check for conflicts before proceeding.

5.2   Expression Validator

As written, the Bison specification in Figure 5.1 will simply evaluate whether the input program matches the desired grammar. `yyparse()` will return zero on success, and non-zero otherwise. Such a program is known as a **validator** and is often used to determine whether a given program is standards compliant.

There are a variety of online validators for web-related languages like HTML[1], CSS[2], and JSON[3]. By having a strict language definition separate from actual implementations (which may contain non-standard features) it is much easier for a programmer to determine whether their code is standards compliant, and therefore (presumably) portable.

---

[1]`http://validator.w3.org`
[2]`http://css-validator.org`
[3]`http://jsonlint.com`

5.3   Expression Interpreter

To do more than simply validate the program, we must make use of **semantic actions** embedded within the grammar itself. Following the right side of any production rule, you may place arbitrary C code inside of curly braces. This code may refer to **semantic values** which represent the values already computed for other non-terminals. Semantic values are given by dollar signs indicating the position of a non-terminal in a production rule. Two dollar signs indicates the semantic value of the current rule.

For example, in the rule for addition, the appropriate semantic action is to add the left value (the first symbol) to the right value (the third symbol):

```
expr : expr TOKEN_PLUS term { $$ = $1 + $3; }
```

Where do the semantic values $1 and $3 come from? They simply come from the other rules that define those non-terminals. Eventually, we reach a rule that gives the value for a leaf node. For example, this rule indicates that the semantic value of an integer token is the integer value of the token text:

```
factor : TOKEN_INT { $$ = atoi(yytext); }
```

(Careful: the value of the token comes from the `yytext` array in the scanner, so you can only do this when the rule has a single terminal on the right hand side of the rule.)

In the cases where a non-terminal expands to a single non-terminal, we simply assign one semantic value to the other:

```
term : factor { $$ = $1; }
```

Because Bison is a bottom-up parser, it determines the semantic values of the leaf nodes in the parse tree first, then passes those up to the interior nodes, and so on until the result reaches the start symbol.

Figure 5.4 shows a Bison grammar that implements a complete interpreter. The main program simply invokes `yyparse()`. If successful, the result is stored in the global variable `parser_result` for extraction and use from the main program.

```
prog : expr TOKEN_SEMI          { parser_result = $1; }
     ;

expr : expr TOKEN_PLUS term         { $$ = $1 + $3; }
     | expr TOKEN_MINUS term        { $$ = $1 - $3; }
     | term                             { $$ = $1; }
     ;

term : term TOKEN_MUL factor        { $$ = $1 * $3; }
     | term TOKEN_DIV factor        { $$ = $1 / $3; }
     | factor                           { $$ = $1; }
     ;

factor
     : TOKEN_MINUS factor                   { $$ = -$2; }
     | TOKEN_LPAREN expr TOKEN_RPAREN   { $$ = $2; }
     | TOKEN_INT                { $$ = atoi(yytext); }
     ;
```

Figure 5.4: Bison Specification for an Interpreter

5.4 Expression Trees

So far, our expression interpreter is computing results in the middle of
parsing the input. While this works for simple expressions, it has several
general drawbacks: One is that the program may perform a large amount
of computation, only to discover a parse error late in the program. It is
generally more desirable to find all parse errors *before* execution.

To fix this, we will add a new stage to the interpreter. Instead of computing values outright, we will construct a data structure known as the
abstract syntax tree to represent the expression. Once the AST is created,
we can traverse the tree to check, execute, and translate the program as
needed.

Figure 5.5 shows the C code for a simple AST representing expressions.
expr_t enumerates the five kinds of expression nodes. struct expr describes a node in the tree, which is described by a kind, a left and right
pointer, and an integer value for a leaf. The function expr_create creates a new tree node of any kind, while expr_create_value creates one
specifically of kind EXPR_VALUE. [4]

---

[4]Although it is verbally awkward, we are using the term "kind" rather than "type", which
will have a very specific meaning later on.

Contents of File: expr.h

```
typedef enum {              struct expr {
    EXPR_ADD,                   expr_t kind;
    EXPR_SUBTRACT,              struct expr *left;
    EXPR_DIVIDE,                struct expr *right;
    EXPR_MULTIPLY,             int value;
    EXPR_VALUE              };
} expr_t;
```

Contents of File: expr.c

```
struct expr * expr_create( expr_t kind,
                           struct expr *left,
                           struct expr *right )
{
    struct expr *e = malloc(sizeof(*e));
    e->kind = kind;
    e->value = 0;
    e->left = left;
    e->right = right;
    return e;
}

struct expr * expr_create_value( int value )
{
    struct expr *e = expr_create(EXPR_VALUE,0,0);
    e->value = value;
    return e;
}
```

Figure 5.5: AST for Expression Interpreter

Using the expression structure, we can create some simple ASTs by hand. For example, if we wanted to create an AST corresponding to the expression (10+20)*30, we could issue this sequence of operations:

```
struct expr *a = expr_create_value(10);
struct expr *b = expr_create_value(20);
struct expr *c = expr_create(EXPR_ADD,a,b);
struct expr *d = expr_create_value(30);
struct expr *e = expr_create(EXPR_MULTIPLY,c,d);
```

Of course, we could have accomplished the same thing by writing a single expression with nested values:

```
struct expr *e =
    expr_create(EXPR_MULTIPLY,
        expr_create(EXPR_ADD,
            expr_create_value(10),
            expr_create value(20)
        ),
        expr_create_value(30)
    );
```

Either way, the result is a data structure like this:

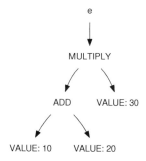

Instead of building each node of the AST by hand, we want Bison to do the same work automatically. As each element of an expression is recognized, a new node in the tree should be created, and passed up so that it can be linked into the appropriate place. By doing a bottom-up parse, Bison will create the leaves of the tree first, and then link them into the parent nodes.

To accomplish this, we must write the semantic actions for each rule to either create a node in the tree, or pass up the pointer from the node below. Figure 5.6 shows how this is done:

```
%{
#include "expr.h"
#define YYSTYPE struct expr *
struct expr * parser_result = 0;
%}

/* token definitions omitted for brevity */

prog : expr TOKEN_SEMI
          { parser_result = $1; }
     ;

expr : expr TOKEN_PLUS term
          { $$ = expr_create(EXPR_ADD,$1,$3); }
     | expr TOKEN_MINUS term
          { $$ = expr_create(EXPR_SUBTRACT,$1,$3); }
     | term
          { $$ = $1; }
     ;

term : term TOKEN_MUL factor
          { $$ = expr_create(EXPR_MULTIPLY,$1,$3); }
     | term TOKEN_DIV factor
          { $$ = expr_create(EXPR_DIVIDE,$1,$3); }
     | factor
          { $$ = $1; }
     ;

factor
     : TOKEN_MINUS factor
          { $$ = expr_create(EXPR_SUBTRACT,
                             expr_create_value(0),$2); }
     | TOKEN_LPAREN expr TOKEN_RPAREN
          { $$ = $2; }
     | TOKEN_INT
          { $$ = expr_create_value(atoi(yytext)); }
     ;
```

Figure 5.6: Building an AST for the Expression Grammar

Examine Figure 5.6 carefully and note several things:

- In the preamble, we must explicitly define the **semantic type** by setting the macro **YYSTYPE** to `struct expr *`. This causes Bison to use `struct expr *` as the internal type everywhere a semantic value such as `$$` or `$1` is used. The final parser result must have the same semantic type, of course.

- The AST does not always correspond directly to the parse tree. For example, where an `expr` produces a `factor`, we simply pass up the pointer to the underlying node with `{$$ = $1;}` On the other hand, when we encounter a unary minus in `term`, we return a subtree that actually implements subtraction between the value zero on the left and the expression on the right.

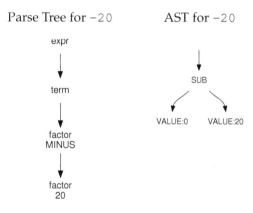

- Parentheses are not directly represented in the AST. Instead, they have the effect of ordering the nodes in the tree to achieve the desired evaluation order. For example, consider the AST generated by these sentences:

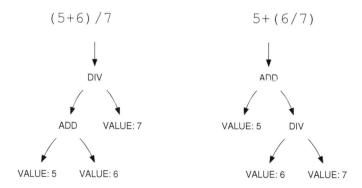

```
int expr_evaluate( struct expr *e )
{
    if(!e) return 0;

    int l = expr_evaluate(e->left);
    int r = expr_evaluate(e->right);

    switch(e->kind) {
        case EXPR_VALUE:    return e->value;
        case EXPR_ADD:      return l+r;
        case EXPR_SUBTRACT: return l-r;
        case EXPR_MULTIPLY: return l*r;
        case EXPR_DIVIDE:
            if(r==0) {
                printf("runtime error: divide by zero\n");
                exit(1);
            }
            return l/r;
    }

    return 0;
}
```

Figure 5.7: Evaluating Expressions

Now that we have constructed the AST, we can use it as the basis for computation and many other operations.

The AST can be evaluated arithmetically by calling expr_evaluate shown in Figure 5.7 This function performs a post-order traversal of the tree by invoking itself recursively on the left and right pointers of the node. (Note the check for a null pointer at the beginning of the function.) Those calls return l and r which contain the integer result of the left and right subtrees. Then, the result of this node is computed by switching on the kind of the current node. (Note also that we must check for division-by-zero explicitly, otherwise expr_evaluate would crash when r is zero.)

```
void expr_print ( struct expr *e )
{
    if(!e) return;

    printf("(");
    expr_print(e->left);

    switch(e->kind) {
        case EXPR_VALUE:     printf("%d",e->value); break;
        case EXPR_ADD:       printf("+"); break;
        case EXPR_SUBTRACT:  printf("-"); break;
        case EXPR_MULTIPLY:  printf("*"); break;
        case EXPR_DIVIDE:    printf("/"); break;
    }

    expr_print(e->right);
    printf(")");
}
```

Figure 5.8: Printing and Evaluating Expressions

In a similar way, the AST can be converted back to text by calling expr_print, shown in Figure 5.8 This function performs an in-order traversal of the expression tree by recursively calling expr_print on the left side of a node, displaying the current node, then calling expr_print on the right side. Again, note the test for null at the beginning of the function.

As noted earlier, parentheses are not directly reflected in the AST. To be conservative, this function displays a parenthesis around every value. While correct, it results in a lot of parentheses! A better solution would be to only print a parenthesis when a subtree contains an operator of lower precedence.

5.5 Exercises

1. Consult the Bison manual and determine how to automatically generate a graph of the LALR automaton from your grammar. Compare the output from Bison against your hand-drawn version.

2. Modify expr_evaluate() (and anything else needed) to handle floating point values instead of integers.

3. Modify expr_print() so that it displays the minimum number of parentheses necessary for correctness.

4. Extend the parser and interpreter to allow for invoking several built-in mathematical functions such as `sin(x)`, `sqrt(x)` and so forth.

   Before coding, think a little bit about where to put the names of the functions. Should they be keywords in the language? Or should any function names be simply treated as identifiers and checked in `expr_evaluate()`?

5. Extend the parser and interpreter to allow for variable assignment and use, so that you can write multiple assignment statements followed by a single expression to be evaluated, like this:

```
g = 9.8;
t = 5;
g*t*t - 7*t + 10;
```

5.6 Further Reading

As its name suggests, YACC was not the first compiler construction tool, but it remains widely used today and has led to a proliferation of similar tools written in various langauges and addressing different classes of grammars. Here is just a small selection:

1. S. C. Johnson, "YACC: Yet Another Compiler-Compiler", Bell Laboratories Technical Journal, 1975.

2. D. Grune and C.J.H Jacobs, "A programmer-friendly LL(1) parser generator", Software: Practice and Experience, volume 18, number 1.

3. T.J. Parr and R.W. Quong, "ANTLR: A predicated LL(k) Parser Generator", Software: Practice and Experience, 1995.

4. S. McPeak, G.C. Necula, "Elkhound: A Fast, Practical GLR Parser Generator", International Conference on Compiler Construction, 2004.

Chapter 6 – The Abstract Syntax Tree

6.1 Overview

The **abstract syntax tree (AST)** is an important internal data structure that represents the primary structure of a program. The AST is the starting point for semantic analysis of a program. It is "abstract" in the sense that the structure leaves out the particular details of parsing: the AST does not care whether a language has prefix, postfix, or infix expressions. (In fact, the AST we describe here can be used to represent most procedural languages.)

For our project compiler, we will define an AST in terms of five C structures representing declarations, statements, expressions, types, and parameters. While you have certainly encountered each of these terms while learning programming, they are not always used precisely in practice. This chapter will help you to sort those items out very clearly:

- A **declaration** states the name, type, and value of a symbol so that it can be used in the program. Symbols included items such as constants, variables, and functions.

- A **statement** indicates an action to be carried out that changes the state of the program. Examples include loops, conditionals, and function returns.

- An **expression** is a combination of values and operations that is **evaluated** according to specific rules and yields a **value** such as an integer, floating point, or string. In some programming languages, an expression may also have a **side effect** that changes the state of the program.

For each kind of element in the AST, we will give an example of the code and how it is constructed. Because each of these structures potentially has pointers to each of the other types, it is necessary to preview all of them before seeing how they work together.

Once you understand all of the elements of the AST, we finish the chapter by demonstrating how the entire structure can be created automatically through the use of the Bison parser generator.

6.2 Declarations

A complete B-Minor program is a sequence of declarations. Each declaration states the existence of a variable or a function. A variable declaration may optionally give an initializing value. If none is given, it is given a default value of zero. A function declaration may optionally give the body of the function in code; if no body is given, then the declaration serves as a prototype for a function declared elsewhere.

For example, the following are all valid declarations:

```
b: boolean;
s: string = "hello";
f: function integer ( x: integer ) = { return x*x; }
```

A declaration is represented by a `decl` structure that gives the name, type, value (if an expression), code (if a function), and a pointer to the next declaration in the program:

```
struct decl {
    char *name;
    struct type *type;
    struct expr *value;
    struct stmt *code;
    struct decl *next;
};
```

Because we will be creating a lot of these structures, you will need a factory function that allocates a structure and initializes its fields, like this:

```
struct decl * decl_create( char *name,
                           struct type *type,
                           struct expr *value,
                           struct stmt *code,
                           struct decl *next )
{
    struct decl *d = malloc(sizeof(*d));
    d->name = name;
    d->type = type;
    d->value = value;
    d->code = code;
    d->next = next;
    return d;
}
```

(You will need to write similar code for statements, expressions, etc, but we won't keep repeating it here.)

The three declarations on the preceding page can be represented graphically as a linked list, like this:

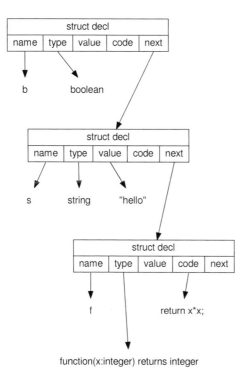

Note that some of the fields point to nothing: these would be represented by a null pointer, which we omit for clarity. Also, our picture is incomplete and must be expanded: the items representing types, expressions, and statements are all complex structures themselves that we must describe.

6.3   Statements

The body of a function consists of a sequence of statements. A statement indicates that the program is to take a particular action in the order specified, such as computing a value, performing a loop, or choosing between branches of an alternative. A statement can also be a declaration of a local variable. Here is the `stmt` structure:

```
struct stmt {                          typedef enum {
    stmt_t kind;                           STMT_DECL,
    struct decl *decl;                     STMT_EXPR,
    struct expr *init_expr;                STMT_IF_ELSE,
    struct expr *expr;                     STMT_FOR,
    struct expr *next_expr;                STMT_PRINT,
    struct stmt *body;                     STMT_RETURN,
    struct stmt *else_body;                STMT_BLOCK
    struct stmt *next;                 } stmt_t;
};
```

The `kind` field indicates what kind of statement it is:

- `STMT_DECL` indicates a (local) declaration, and the `decl` field will point to it.

- `STMT_EXPR` indicates an expression statement and the `expr` field will point to it.

- `STMT_IF_ELSE` indicates an if-else expression such that the `expr` field will point to the control expression, the `body` field to the statements executed if it is true, and the `else_body` field to the statements executed if it is false.

- `STMT_FOR` indicates a for-loop, such that `init_expr`, `expr`, and `next_expr` are the three expressions in the loop header, and `body` points to the statements in the loop.

- `STMT_PRINT` indicates a `print` statement, and `expr` points to the expressions to print.

- `STMT_RETURN` indicates a `return` statement, and `expr` points to the expression to return.

- `STMT_BLOCK` indicates a block of statements inside curly braces, and `body` points to the contained statements.

And, as we did with declarations, we require a function `stmt_create` to create and return a statement structure:

```
struct stmt * stmt_create( stmt_t kind,
    struct decl *decl, struct expr *init_expr,
    struct expr *expr, struct expr *next_expr,
    struct stmt *body, struct stmt *else_body,
    struct stmt *next );
```

This structure has a lot of fields, but each one serves a purpose and is used when necessary for a particular kind of statement. For example, an if-else statement only uses the `expr`, `body`, and `else_body` fields, leaving the rest null:

`if( x<y ) print x; else print y;`

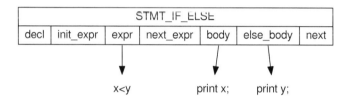

A for-loop uses the three `expr` fields to represent the thre parts of the loop control, and the `body` field to represent the code being executed:

`for(i=0;i<10;i++) print i;`

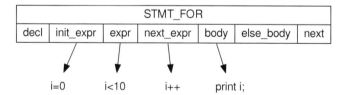

6.4 Expressions

Expressions are implemented much like the simple expression AST shown in Chapter 5. The difference is that we need many more binary types: one for every operator in the language, including arithmetic, logical, comparison, assignment, and so forth. We also need one for every type of leaf value, including variable names, constant values, and so forth. The name field will be set for EXPR_NAME, the integer_value field for EXPR_INTEGER_LITERAL, and so on. You may need to add values and types to this structure as you expand your compiler.

```
struct expr {                      typedef enum {
    expr_t kind;                       EXPR_ADD,
    struct expr *left;                 EXPR_SUB,
    struct expr *right;                EXPR_MUL,
                                       EXPR_DIV,
    const char *name;                  ...
    int integer_value;                 EXPR_NAME,
    const char * string_literal;       EXPR_INTEGER_LITERAL,
};                                     EXPR_STRING_LITERAL
                                   } expr_t;
```

As before, you should create a factory for a binary operator:

```
struct expr * expr_create( expr_t kind,
                           struct expr *L, struct expr *R );
```

And then a factory for each of the leaf types:

```
struct expr * expr_create_name( const char *name );
struct expr * expr_create_integer_literal( int i );
struct expr * expr_create_boolean_literal( int b );
struct expr * expr_create_char_literal( char c );
struct expr * expr_create_string_literal( const char *str );
```

Note that you can store the integer, boolean, and character literal values all in the integer_value field.

A few cases deserve special mention. Unary operators like logical-not typically have their sole argument in the `left` pointer:

A function call is constructed by creating an EXPR_CALL node, such that the left-hand side is the function name, and the right hand side is an unbalanced tree of EXPR_ARG nodes. While this looks a bit awkward, it allows us to express a linked list using a tree, and will simplify the handling of function call arguments on the stack during code generation.

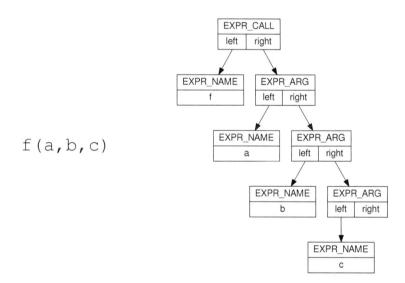

Array subscripting is treated like a binary operator, such that the name of the array is on the left side of the EXPR_SUBSCRIPT operator, and an integer expression on the right:

a[b]

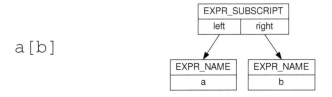

6.5 Types

A type structure encodes the type of every variable and function mentioned in a declaration. Primitive types like integer and boolean are expressed by simply setting the kind field appropriately, and leaving the other fields null. Compound types like array and function are built by connecting multiple type structures together.

```
typedef enum {
    TYPE_VOID,
    TYPE_BOOLEAN,
    TYPE_CHARACTER,
    TYPE_INTEGER,
    TYPE_STRING,
    TYPE_ARRAY,
    TYPE_FUNCTION
} type_t;

struct type {
    type_t kind;
    struct type *subtype;
    struct param_list *params;
};

struct param_list {
    char *name;
    struct type *type;
    struct param_list *next;
};
```

For example, to express a basic type like a boolean or an integer, we simply create a standalone `type` structure, with `kind` set appropriately, and the other fields null:

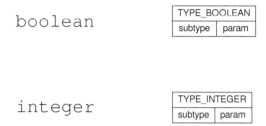

To express a compound type like an array of integers, we set `kind` to TYPE_ARRAY and set `subtype` to point to a TYPE_INTEGER:

These can be linked to arbitrary depth, so to express an array of array of integers:

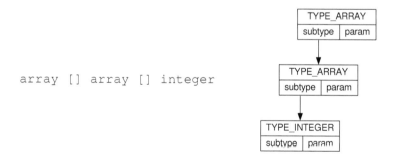

To express the type of a function, we use `subtype` to express the return type of the function, and then connect a linked list of `param_list` nodes to describe the name and type of each parameter to the function.

For example, here is the type of a function which takes two arguments and returns an integer:

```
function integer (s:string, c:char)
```

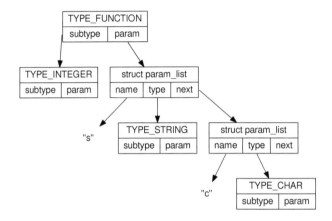

Note that the type structures here let us express some complicated and powerful higher order concepts of programming. By simply swapping in complex types, you can describe an array of ten functions, each returning an integer:

```
a: array [10] function integer ( x: integer );
```

Or how about a function that returns a function?

```
f: function function integer (x:integer) (y:integer);
```

Or even a function that returns an array of functions!

```
g: function array [10]
        function integer (x:integer) (y:integer);
```

While the B-Minor type system is capable of *expressing* these ideas, these combinations will be rejected later in typechecking, because they require a more dynamic implementation than we are prepared to create. If you find these ideas interesting, then you should read up on functional languages such as Scheme and Haskell.

6.6 Putting it All Together

Now that you have seen each individual component, let's see how a complete B-Minor function would be expressed as an AST:

```
compute: function integer ( x:integer ) = {
        i: integer;
        total: integer = 0;
        for(i=0;i<10;i++) {
                total = total + i;
        }
        return total;
}
```

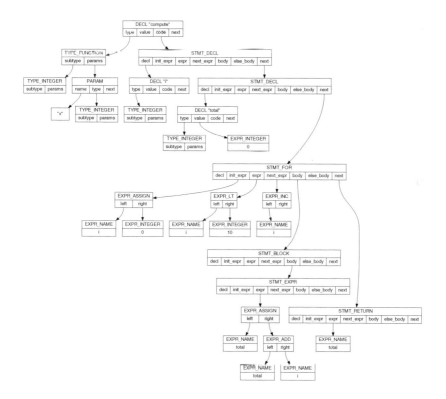

6.7   Building the AST

With the functions created so far in this chapter, we could, in principle, construct the AST manually in a sort of nested style,. For example, the following code represents a function called `square` which accepts an integer x as a parameter, and returns the value x*x:

```
d = decl_create(
    "square",
    type_create(TYPE_FUNCTION,
        type_create(TYPE_INTEGER,0,0),
        param_list_create(
            "x",
            type_create(TYPE_INTEGER,0,0)
            0)),
    0,
    stmt_create(STMT_RETURN,0,0,
        expr_create(EXPR_MUL,
            expr_create_name("x"),
            expr_create_name("x")),
        0,0,0,0),
    0);
```

Obviously, this is no way to write code! Instead, we want our parser to invoke the various creation functions whenever they are reduced, and then hook them up into a complete tree. Using an LR parser generator like Bison, this process is straightforward. (Here I will give you the idea of how to proceed, but you will need to figure out many of the details in order to complete the parser.)

At the top level, a B-Minor program is a sequence of declarations:

```
program : decl_list
            { parser_result = $1; }
        ;
```

Then, we write rules for each of the various kinds of declarations in a B-Minor program:

```
decl : name TOKEN_COLON type TOKEN_SEMI
        { $$ = decl_create($1,$3,0,0,0); }
     | name TOKEN_COLON type TOKEN_ASSIGN expr TOKEN_SEMI
        { $$ = decl_create($1,$3,$5,0,0); }
     | /* and more cases here */
           . . .
     ;
```

Since each `decl` structure is created separately, we must connect them together in a linked list formed by a `decl_list`. This is most easily done by making the rule right-recursive, so that `decl` on the left represents one declaration, and `decl_list` on the right represents the remainder of the linked list. The end of the list is a null value provided when `decl_list` produces ϵ.

```
decl_list : decl decl_list
              { $$ = $1; $1->next = $2; }
            | /* epsilon */
              { $$ = 0; }
            ;
```

For each kind of statement, we create a `stmt` structure that pulls out the necessary elements from the grammar.

```
stmt : TOKEN_IF TOKEN_LPAREN expr TOKEN_RPAREN stmt
         { $$ = stmt_create(STMT_IF_ELSE,0,0,$3,0,$5,$0,0); }
       | TOKEN_LBRACE stmt_list TOKEN_RBRACE
         { $$ = stmt_create(STMT_BLOCK,0,0,0,0,$2,0,0); }
       | /* and more cases here */
         . . .
       ;
```

Proceed in this way down through each of the grammar elements of a B-Minor program: declarations, statements, expressions, types, parameters, until you reach the leaf elements of literal values and symbols, which are handled in the same way as in Chapter 5.

There is one last complication: What, exactly is the semantic type of the values returned as each rule is reduced? It isn't a single type, because each kind of rule returns a different data structure: a declaration rule returns a `struct decl *`, while an identifier rule returns a `char *`. To make this work, we inform Bison that the semantic value is the union of all of the types in the AST:

```
%union {
        struct decl *decl;
        struct stmt *stmt;
        . . .
        char *name;
};
```

And then indicate the specific subfield of the union used by each rule:

```
%type <decl> program decl_list decl . . .
%type <stmt> stmt_list stmt . . .
. . .
%type <name> name
```

6.8   Exercises

1. Write a complete LR grammar for B-Minor and test it using Bison. Your first attempt will certainly have many shift-reduce and reduce-reduce conflicts, so use your knowledge of grammars from Chapter 4 to rewrite the grammar and eliminate the conflicts.

2. Write the AST structures and generating functions as outlined in this chapter, and manually construct some simple ASTs using nested function calls as shown above.

3. Add new functions `decl_print()`, `stmt_print()`, etc. that print the AST back out so you can verify that the program was generated correctly. Make your output nicely formatted using indentation and consistent spacing, so that the code is easily readable.

4. Add the AST generator functions as action rules to your Bison grammar, so that you can parse complete programs, and print them back out again.

5. Add new functions `decl_translate()`, `stmt_translate()`, etc. that output the B-Minor AST in a different language of your own choosing, such as Python or Java or Rust.

6. Add new functions that emit the AST in a graphical form so you can "see" the structure of a program. One approach would be to use the Graphviz DOT format: let each declaration, statement, etc be a node in a graph, and then let each pointer between structures be an edge in the graph.

Chapter 7 – Semantic Analysis

Now that we have completed construction of the AST, we are ready to begin analyzing the **semantics**, or the actual meaning of a program, and not simply its structure.

Type checking is a major component of semantic analysis. Broadly speaking, the type system of a programming language gives the programmer a way to make verifiable assertions that the compiler can check automatically. This allows for the detection of errors at compile-time, instead of at runtime.

Different programming languages have different approaches to type checking. Some languages (like C) have a rather weak type system, so it is possible to make serious errors if you are not careful. Other languages (like Ada) have very strong type systems, but this makes it more difficult to write a program that will compile at all!

Before we can perform type checking, we must determine the type of each identifier used in an expression. However, the mapping between variable names and their actual storage locations is not immediately obvious. A variable x in an expression could refer to a local variable, a function parameter, a global variable, or something else entirely. We solve this problem by performing **name resolution**, in which each definition of a variable is entered into a **symbol table**. This table is referenced throughout the semantic analysis stage whenever we need to evaluate the correctness of some code.

Once name resolution is completed, we have all the information necessary to check types. In this stage, we compute the type of complex expressions by combining the basic types of each value according to standard conversion rules. If a type is used in a way that is not permitted, the compiler will output an (ideally helpful) error message that will assist the programmer in resolving the problem.

Semantic analysis also includes other forms of checking the correctness of a program, such as examining the limits of arrays, avoiding bad pointer traversals, and examining control flow. Depending on the design of the language, some of these problems can be detected at compile time, while others may need to wait until runtime.

7.1   Overview of Type Systems

Most programming languages assign to every value (whether a literal, constant, or variable) a **type**, which describes the interpretation of the data in that variable: Is it an integer, a floating point number, a boolean, a string, a pointer, or something else? In most languages, these atomic types can be combined into higher-order types such as enumerations, structures, and variant types to express complex constraints.

The type system of a language serves several purposes:

- **Correctness.** A compiler uses type information provided by the programmer to raise warnings or errors if a program attempts to do something improper. For example, it is almost certainly an error to assign an integer value to a pointer variable, even though both might be implemented as a single word in memory. A good type system can help to eliminate runtime errors by flagging them at compile time instead.

- **Performance.** A compiler can use type information to find the most efficient implementation of a piece of code. For example, if the programmer tells the compiler that a given variable is a constant, then the same value can be loaded into a register and used many times, rather than constantly loading it from memory.

- **Expressiveness.** A program can be made more compact and expressive if the language allows the programmer to leave out facts that can be inferred from the type system. For example, in B-Minor , the print statement does not need to be told whether it is printing an integer, a string, or a boolean: the type is inferred from the expression and the value is automatically displayed in the proper way.

A programming language (and its type system) are commonly classified on the following axes:

- safe or unsafe

- static or dynamic

- explicit or implicit

In an **unsafe programming language**, it is possible to write valid programs that have wildly undefined behavior that violates the basic structure of the program. For example, in the C programming language, a program can construct an arbitrary pointer to modify any word in memory, and thereby change the data and code of the compiled program. Such power is probably necessary to implement low-level code like an operating system or a driver, but is problematic for general applications code.

For example, the following code in C is syntactically legal and will compile, but is unsafe because it writes data outside the bounds of the array a[]. As a result, the program could have almost any outcome, including incorrect output, silent data corruption, or an infinite loop.

```
/* This is C code */
int i;
int a[10];
for(i=0;i<100;i++) a[i] = i;
```

In a **safe programming language**, it is not possible to write a program that violates the basic structures of the language. That is, no matter what input is given to a program written in a safe language, it will always execute in a well defined way that preserves the abstractions of the language. A safe programming language enforces the boundaries of arrays, the use of pointers, and the assignment of types to prevent undefined behavior. Most interpreted languages, like Perl, Python, and Java, are safe languages.

For example, in C#, the boundaries of arrays are checked at runtime, so that running off the end of an array has the predicable effect of throwing an IndexOutOfRangeException:

```
/* This is C-sharp code */
a = new int[10];
for(int i=0;i<100;i++) a[i] = i;
```

In a **statically typed language**, all typechecking is performed at compile-time, long before the program runs. This means that the program can be translated into basic machine code without retaining any of the type information, because all operations have been checked and determined to be safe. This yields the most high performance code, but does eliminate some kinds of convenient programming idioms.

Static typing is often used to distinguish between integer and floating point operations. While operations like addition and multiplication are usually represented by the same symbols in the source language, they are implemented with fundamentally different machine code. For example, in the C language on X86 machines, (a+b) would be translated to an ADDL instruction for integers, but an FMUL instruction for floating point values. To know which instruction to apply, we must first determine the type of a and b and deduce the intended meaning of +.

In a **dynamically typed language**, type information is available at runtime, and stored in memory alongside the data that it describes. As the program executes, the safety of each operation is checked by comparing the types of each operand. If types are observed to be incompatible, then the program must halt with a runtime type error. This also allows for code that can explicitly examine the type of a variable. For example, the `instanceof` operator in Java allows one to test for types explicitly:

```
/* This is Java code */

public void sit( Furniture f ) {
    if (f instanceof Chair) {
        System.out.println("Sit up straight!\n");
    } else if ( f instanceof Couch ) {
        System.out.println("You may slouch.\n");
    } else {
        System.out.println("You may sit normally.\n");
    }
}
```

In an **explicitly typed language**, the programmer is responsible for indicating the types of variables and other items in the code explicitly. This requires more effort on the programmer's part, but reduces the possibility of unexpected errors. For example, in an explicitly typed language like C, the following code might result in an error or warning, due to the loss of precision when assigning a floating point to an integer:[1]

```
/* This is C code */
int x = 32.5;
```

Explicit typing can also be used to prevent assignment between variables that have the same underlying representation, but different meaning. For example, in C and C++, pointers to different types have the same implementation (a pointer) but it makes no sense to interchange them. The following should generate an error or at least a warning:

```
/* This is C code */
int *i;
float *f = i;
```

In an **implicitly typed language**, the compiler will infer the type of variables and expressions (to the degree possible) without explicit input from the programmer. This allows for programs to be more compact, but can result in accidental behavior. For example, recent C++ standards now allow a variable to be declared with automatic type `auto`, like this:

```
/* This is C++11 code */
auto x = 32.5;
cout << x << endl;
```

---

[1]Not all C compilers will generate a warning, but they should!

The compiler determines that 32.5 has type `double`, and therefore x must also have type `double`. In a similar way, the output operator $<<$ is defined to have a certain behavior on integers, another behavior on strings, and so forth. In this case, the compiler already determined that the type of x is `double` and so it chooses the variant of $<<$ that operates on doubles.

7.2 Designing a Type System

To describe the type system of a language, we must explain its atomic types, its compound types, and the rules for assigning and converting between types.

The **atomic types** of a language are the simple types used to describe individual variables that are typically (though not always) stored in single registers in assembly language: integers, floating point numbers, boolean values, and so forth. For each atomic type, it is necessary to clearly define the range that is supported. For example, integers may be signed or unsigned, be 8 or 16 or 32 or 64 bits; floating point numbers could be 32 or 40 or 64 bits; characters could be ASCII or Unicode.

Many languages allow for **user-defined types** in which the programmer defines a new type that is implemented using an atomic type, but gives it a new meaning by restricting the range. For example, in Ada, you might define new types for days and months:

```
-- This is Ada code
type Day is range 1..31;
type Month is range 1..12;
```

This is useful because variables and functions dealing with days and months are now kept separate, preventing you from accidentally assigning one to another, or for giving the value 13 to a variable of type `Month`.

C has a similar feature, but it is much weaker: `typedef` declares a new name for a type, but doesn't have any means of restricting the range, and doesn't prevent you from making assignments between types that share the same base type:

```
/* This is C code */
typedef int Month;
typedef int Day;

/* Assigning m to d is allowed in C,
   because they are both integers. */

Month m = 10;
Day d = m;
```

Enumerations are another kind of user-defined type in which the programmer indicates a finite set of symbolic values that a variable can contain. For example, if you are working with uncertain boolean variables in Rust, you might declare:

```
/* This is Rust code */
enum Fuzzy { True, False, Uncertain };
```

Internally, an enumeration value is simply an integer, but it makes the source code more readable, and also allows the compiler to prevent the programmer from assigning an illegal value. Once again, the C language allows you to declare enumerations, but doesn't prevent you from mixing and matching integers and enumerations.

The **compound types** of a language combine together existing types into more complex aggregations. You are surely familiar with a **structure type** (or **record type**) that groups together several values into a larger whole. For example, you might group together latitude and longitude to treat them as a single `coordinate`:

```
/* This is Go code */
type coordinates struct {
    latitude float64
    longitude float64
}
```

Less frequently used are **union types** in which multiple symbols occupy the same memory. For example, in C, you can declare a union type of `number` that contains an overlapping float and integer:

```
/* This is C code */
union number {
int i;
float f;
};

union number n;
n.i = 10;
n.f = 3.14;
```

In this case, `n.i` and `n.f` occupy the same memory. If you assign `10` to `n.i` and read it back, you will see `10` as expected. However, if you assign `10` to `n.i` and read back `n.f`, you will likely observe a garbage value, depending on how exactly the two values are mapped into memory. Union types are occasionally handy when implementing operating system features such as device drivers, because hardware interfaces often re-use the same memory locations for multiple purposes.

Some languages provide a **variant type** which allows the programmer to explicitly describe a type with multiple variants, each with different fields. This is similar to the concept of a union type, but prevents the programmer from performing unsafe accesses. For example, Rust allows us to create a variant type representing an expression tree:

```
/* This is Rust code */
enum Expression {
    ADD{ left: Expression, right: Expression },
    MULTIPLY{ left: Expression, right: Expression },
    INTEGER{ value: i32 },
    NAME{ name: string }
}
```

This variant type is tightly controlled so that it is difficult to use incorrectly. For an Expression of type ADD, it has `left` and `right` fields which can be used in the expected way. For an Expression of type NAME, the name field can be used. The other fields are simply not available unless the appropriate type is selected.

Finally, we must define what happens when unlike types are used together. Suppose that an integer i is assigned to a floating point f. A similar question arises when an integer is passed to a function expecting a floating point as an argument. There are several possibilities for what a language may do in this case:

- **Disallow the assignment.** A very strict language (like B-Minor) could simply emit an error and prevent the program from compiling! Perhaps it simply makes no sense to make the assignment, and the compiler is saving the programmer from a grievous error. If the assignment is *really* desired, it could be accomplished by requiring that the programmer call a built-in conversion function (e.g. `IntToFloat`) that accepts one type and returns another.

- **Perform a bitwise copy.** If the two variables have the same underlying storage size, the unlike assignment could be accomplished by just copying the bits in one variable to the location of the other. This is *usually* a bad idea, since there is no guarantee that one data type has any meaning in the other context. But it does happen in a few select cases, such as when assigning different pointer types in C.

- **Convert to an equivalent value.** For certain types, the compiler may have built-in conversions that change the value to the desired type implicitly. For example, it is common to implicitly convert between integers and floating points, or between signed and unsigned integers. But this does not mean the operation is safe! An implied conversion can lose information, resulting in very tricky bugs.

- **Interpret the value in a different way.** In some cases, it may be desirable to convert the value into some other value that is not equivalent, but still useful for the programmer. For example, in Perl, when a list is copied to a scalar context, the *length* of the list is placed in the target variable, rather than the content of the list.

```
@days = ("Monday", "Tuesday", "Wednesday", ... );
@a = @days; # copies the array to array a
$b = @days; # puts the length of the array into b
```

7.3   The B-Minor Type System

The B-Minor type system is safe, static, and explicit. As a result, it is fairly compact to describe, and straightforward to implement, and will eliminate a large number of programming errors. However, it may be more strict than some languages, so there s going to be a large number of errors that we must detect.

B-Minor has the following atomic types:

- `integer` - A 64 bit signed integer.

- `boolean` - Limited to symbols `true` or `false`.

- `char` - Limited to ASCII values.

- `string` - ASCII values, null terminated.

- `void` - Only used for a function that returns no value.

And the following compound types:

- `array [size] type`

- `function type ( a:  type, b:  type, ...  )`

And here are the type rules that must be enforced:

- A value may only be assigned to a variable of the same type.

- A function parameter may only accept a value of the same type.

- The type of a `return` statement must match the function return type.

- All binary operators must have the same type on the left and right hand sides.

- The equality operators `!=` and `==` may be applied to any type except `void`, `array`, or `function` and always return `boolean`.

- The comparison operators < <= >= > may only be applied to `integer` values and always return `boolean`.

- The boolean operators ! && || may only be applied to `boolean` values and always return `boolean`.

- The arithmetic operators + - * / % ^ ++ -- may only be applied to `integer` values and always return `integer`.

7.4 The Symbol Table

The **symbol table** records all of the information that we need to know about every declared variable (and other named items, like functions) in the program. Each entry in the table is a `struct symbol` which is shown in Figure 7.1.

```
struct symbol {                 typedef enum {
    symbol_t kind;                  SYMBOL_LOCAL,
    struct type *type;              SYMBOL_PARAM,
    char *name;                     SYMBOL_GLOBAL
    int which;                  } symbol_t;
};
```

Figure 7.1: The Symbol Structure

The `kind` field indicates whether the symbol is a local variable, a global variable, or a function parameter. The `type` field points to a type structure indicating the type of the variable. The `name` field gives the name (obviously), and the `which` field gives the ordinal position of local variables and parameters. (More on that later.)

As with all the other data structures we have created so far, we must have a factory function like this:

```
struct symbol * symbol_create( symbol_t kind,
                               struct type *type,
                               char *name ) {
    struct symbol *s = malloc(sizeof(*s));
    s->kind = kind;
    s->type = type;
    s->name = name;
    return s;
}
```

To begin semantic analysis, we must create a suitable `symbol` structure for each variable declaration, and enter it into the symbol table.

Conceptually, the symbol table is just a map between the name of each variable, and the symbol structure that describes it:

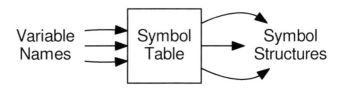

However, it's not *quite* that simple, because most programming languages allow the same variable name to be used multiple times, as long as each definition is in a distinct **scope**. In C-like languages (including B-Minor) there is a global scope, a scope for function parameters and local variables, and then nested scopes everywhere curly braces appear.

For example, the following B-Minor program defines the symbol x three times, each with a different type and storage class. When run, the program should print 10 hello false.

```
x: integer = 10;

f: function void ( x: string ) =
{
    print x, "\n";
    {
        x: boolean = false;
        print x, "\n";
    }
}

main: function void () =
{
    print x, "\n";
    f("hello");
}
```

To accommodate these multiple definitions, we will structure our symbol table as a stack of hash tables, as shown in Figure 7.2. Each hash table maps the names in a given scope to their corresponding symbols. This allows a symbol (like x) to exist in multiple scopes without conflict. As we proceed through the program, we will push a new table every time a scope is entered, and pop a table every time a scope is left.

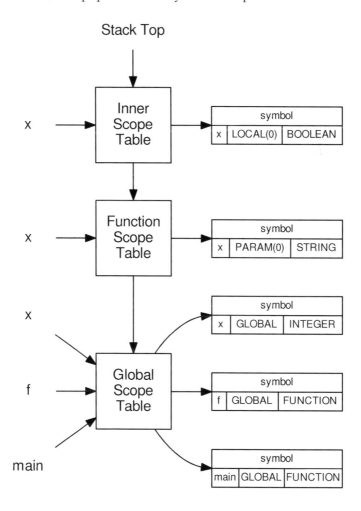

Figure 7.2: A Nested Symbol Table

```
void scope_enter();
void scope_exit();
int  scope_level();

void scope_bind( const char *name, struct symbol *sym );
struct symbol * scope_lookup( const char *name );
struct symbol * scope_lookup_current( const char *name );
```

Figure 7.3: Symbol Table API

To manipulate the symbol table, we define six operations in the API given in Figure 7.3. They have the following meaning:

- `scope_enter()` causes a new hash table to be pushed on the top of the stack, representing a new scope.

- `scope_leave()` causes the topmost hash table to be removed.

- `scope_level()` returns the number of hash tables in the current stack. (This is helpful to know whether we are at the global scope or not.)

- `scope_bind(name, sym)` adds an entry to the topmost hash table of the stack, mapping name to the symbol structure `sym`.

- `scope_lookup(name)` searches the stack of hash tables from top to bottom, looking for the first entry that matches name exactly. if no match is found, it returns null.

- `scope_lookup_current(name)` works like `scope_lookup` except that it only searches the topmost table. This is used to determine whether a symbol has already been defined in the current scope.

7.5 Name Resolution

With the symbol table in place, we are now ready to match each use of a variable name to its matching definition. This process is known as **name resolution**. To implement name resolution, we will write a `resolve` method for each of the structures in the AST, including `decl_resolve()`, `stmt_resolve()` and so forth.

Collectively, these methods must iterate over the entire AST, looking for variable declarations and uses. Wherever a variable is declared, it must be entered into the symbol table and the `symbol` structure linked into the AST. Wherever a variable is used, it must be looked up in the symbol table, and the `symbol` structure linked into the AST. Of course, if a symbol is declared twice in the same scope, or used without declaration, then an appropriate error message must be emitted.

We will begin with declarations, as shown in Figure 7.4. Each `struct decl` represents a variable declaration of some kind, so `decl_resolve` will create a new symbol, and then bind it to the name of the declaration in the current scope. If the declaration represents an expression (`d->value` is not null) then the expression should be resolved. If the declaration represents a function (`d->code` is not null) then we must create a new scope and resolve the parameters and the code.

Figure 7.4 gives some sample code for resolving declarations. As always in this book, consider this starter code in order to give you the basic idea. You will have to make some changes in order to accommodate all the features of the language, handle errors cleanly, and so forth.

In a similar fashion, we must write resolve methods for each structure in the AST. `stmt_resolve()` (not shown) must simply call the appropriate `resolve` on each of its sub-components. In the case of a STMT_BLOCK, it must also enter and leave a new scope. `param_list_resolve()` (also not shown) must enter a new variable declaration for each parameter of a function, so that those definitions are available to the code of a function.

To perform name resolution on the entire AST, you may simply invoke `decl_resolve()` once on the root node of the AST. This function will traverse the entire tree by calling the necessary sub-functions.

```
void decl_resolve( struct decl *d )
{
    if(!d) return;

    symbol_t kind = scope_level() > 1 ?
                    SYMBOL_LOCAL : SYMBOL_GLOBAL;

    d->symbol = symbol_create(kind,d->type,d->name);

    expr_resolve(d->value);
    scope_bind(d->name,d->symbol);

    if(d->code) {
        scope_enter();
        param_list_resolve(d->type->params);
        stmt_resolve(d->code);
        scope_exit();
    }

    decl_resolve(d->next);
}
```

Figure 7.4: Name Resolution for Declarations

```
void expr_resolve( struct expr *e )
{
    if(!e) return;

    if( e->kind==EXPR_NAME ) {
        e->symbol = scope_lookup(e->name);
    } else {
        expr_resolve( e->left );
        expr_resolve( e->right );
    }
}
```

Figure 7.5: Name Resolution for Expressions

7.6   Implementing Type Checking

Before checking expressions, we need some helper functions for checking and manipulating type structures. Here is pseudo-code for checking
equality, copying, and deleting types:

```
int type_equals( struct type *a, struct type *b )
{
    if( a->kind == b->kind ) {
        if( a and b are atomic types ){
            Return true;
        } else if ( both are array ) {
            Return true if subtype is recursively equal
        } else if ( both are function ) {
            Return true if both subtype and params
            are recursively equal
        }
    } else {
        return false;
    }
}

struct type * type_copy( struct type *t )
{
    Return a duplicate copy of t, making sure
    to duplicate subtype and params recursively.
}

void type_delete( struct type *t )
{
    Free all the elements of t recursively.
}
```

Next, we construct a function expr_typecheck that will compute the
proper type of an expression, and return it. To simplify our code, we assert
that expr_typecheck, if called on a non-null expr, will always return
a newly-allocated type structure. If the expression contains an invalid
combination of types, then expr_typecheck will print out an error, but
return a valid type, so that the compiler can continue on and find as many
errors as possible.

The general approach is to perform a recursive, post-order traversal of
the expression tree. At the leaves of the tree, the type of the node simply
corresponds to the kind of the expression node: an integer literal has integer type, a string literal has string type, and so on. If we encounter a variable name, the type can be determined by following the symbol pointer

to the symbol structure, which contains the type. This type is copied and returned to the parent node.

For interior nodes of the expression tree, we must compare the type of the left and right subtrees, and determine if they are compatible with the rules indicated in Section 7.3. If not, we emit an error message and increment a global error counter. Either way, we return the appropriate type for the operator. The types of the left and right branches are no longer needed and can be deleted before returning.

Here is the basic code structure:

```
struct type * expr_typecheck( struct expr *e )
{
    if(!e) return 0;

    struct type *lt = expr_typecheck(e->left);
    struct type *rt = expr_typecheck(e->right);

    struct type *result;

    switch(e->kind) {
        case EXPR_INTEGER_LITERAL:
            result = type_create(TYPE_INTEGER,0,0);
            break;
        case EXPR_STRING_LITERAL:
            result = type_create(TYPE_STRING,0,0);
            break;


        /* more cases here */


    }

    type_delete(lt);
    type_delete(rt);

    return result;
}
```

Let's consider the cases for a few operators in detail. Arithmetic operators can only be applied to integers, and always return an integer type:

```
case EXPR_ADD:
    if( lt->kind != TYPE_INTEGER || rt->kind!=TYPE_INTEGER ) {
        /* display an error */
    }
    result = type_create(TYPE_INTEGER,0,0);
    break;
```

The equality operators can be applied to most types, as long as the types are equal on both sides. These always return boolean.

```
case EXPR_EQ:
case EXPR_NE:
    if(!type_equals(lt,rt)) {
        /* display an error */
    }
    if(lt->kind==TYPE_VOID ||
       lt->kind==TYPE_ARRAY ||
       lt->kind==TYPE_FUNCTION) {
        /* display an error */
    }
    result = type_create(TYPE_BOOLEAN,0,0);
    break;
```

An array derefence like a[i] requires that a be an array, i be an integer, and returns the subtype of the array:

```
case EXPR_DEREF:
    if(lt->kind==TYPE_ARRAY) {
        if(rt->kind!=TYPE_INTEGER) {
            /* error: index not an integer */
        }
        result = type_copy(lt->subtype);
    } else {
        /* error: not an array */
        /* but we need to return a valid type */
        result = type_copy(lt);
    }
    break;
```

Most of the hard work in typechecking is done in expr_typecheck, but we still need to implement typechecking on declarations, statements, and the other elements of the AST. decl_typecheck, stmt_typecheck and the other typechecking methods simply traverse the AST, compute the type of expressions, and then check them against declarations and other constraints as needed.

For example, `decl_typecheck` simply confirms that variable declarations match their initializers and otherwise typechecks the body of function declarations:

```
void decl_typecheck( struct decl *d )
{
    if( d->value ) {
struct type *t;
        t = expr_typecheck(d->value);
        if(!type_equals(t,d->symbol->type)) {
            /* display an error */
        }
    }
    if(d->code) {
        stmt_typecheck(d->code);
    }
}
```

Statements must be typechecked by evaluating each of their components, and then verifying that types match where needed. After the type is examined, it is no longer needed and may be deleted. For example, if-then statements require that the control expression have boolean type:

```
void stmt_typecheck( struct stmt *s )
{
    struct type *t;
    switch(s->kind) {
        case STMT_EXPR:
            t = expr_typecheck(s->expr);
            type_delete(t);
            break;
        case STMT_IF_THEN:
            t = expr_typecheck(s->expr);
            if(t->kind!=TYPE_BOOLEAN) {
                /* display an error */
            }
            type_delete(t);
            stmt_typecheck(s->body);
            stmt_typecheck(s->else_body);
            break;

        /* more cases here */
    }
}
```

7.7 Error Messages

Compilers in general are notorious for displaying terrible error messages. Fortunately, we have developed enough code structure that it is straightforward to display an informative error message that explains exactly what types were discovered, and what the problem is.

For example, this bit of B-Minor code has a mess of type problems:

```
s: string = "hello";
b: boolean = false;
i: integer = s + (b<5);
```

Most compilers would emit an unhelpful message like this:

```
error: type compatibility in expression
```

But, your project compiler can very easily have much more detailed error messages like this:

```
error: cannot compare a boolean (b) to an integer (5)
error: cannot add a boolean (b<5) to a string (s)
```

It's just a matter of taking some care in printing out each of the expressions and types involved when a problem is found:

```
printf("error: cannot add a ");
type_print(lt);
printf(" (");
expr_print(e->left);
printf(") to a ");
type_print(rt);
printf(" (");
expr_print(e->right);
printf(")\n");
```

7.8 Exercises

1. Implement the symbol and scope functions in `symbol.c` and `scope.c`, using an existing hash table implementation as a starting point.

2. Complete the name resolution code by writing `stmt_resolve()` and `param_list_resolve()` and any other supporting code needed.

3. Modify `decl_resolve()` and `expr_resolve()` to display errors when the same name is declared twice, or when a variables is used without a declaration.

4. Complete the implementation of `expr_typecheck` so that it checks and returns the type of all kinds of expressions.

5. Complete the implementation of `stmt_typecheck` by enforcing the constraints particularly to each kind of statement.

6. Write a function `myprintf` that displays printf-style format strings, but supports symbols like `%T` for types, `%E` for expressions, and so forth. This will make it easier to emit error messages, like this:

   ```
   myprintf("error: cannot add a %T (%E) to a %T (%E)\n",
            lt,e->left,rt,e->right);
   ```

   Consult a standard C manual and learn about the functions in the `stdarg.h` header for creating variadic functions.

7.9 Further Reading

1. H. Abelson, G. Sussman, and J. Sussman, "Structure and Interpretation of Computer Programs", MIT press, 1996.

2. B. Pierce, "Types and Programming Languages", MIT Press, 2002.

3. D. Friedman and D. Christiansen, "The Little Typer", MIT Press, 2018.

Chapter 8 – Intermediate Representations

8.1 Introduction

Most production compilers make use of an **intermediate representation (IR)** that lies somewhere between the abstract structure of the source language and the concrete structure of the target assembly language.

An IR is designed to have a simple and regular structure that facilitates optimization, analysis, and efficient code generation. A modular compiler will often implement each optimization or analysis tool as a separate module that consumes and produces the same IR, so that it is easy to select and compose optimizations in different orders.

It is common for an IR to have a defined **external format** that can be written out to a file in text form, so that it can be exchanged between unrelated tools. Although it may be visible to the determined programmer, it usually isn't meant to be easily readable. When loaded into memory, the IR is represented as a data structure, to facilitate algorithms that traverse its structure.

There are many different kinds of IR that can be used; some are very close to the AST we used up to this point, while others are only a very short distance from the target assembly language. Some compilers even use multiple IRs in decreasing layers of abstraction. In this chapter, we will examine different approaches to IRs and consider their strengths and weaknesses.

8.2 Abstract Syntax Tree

First, we will point out that the AST itself can be a usable IR, if the goal is simply to emit assembly language without a great deal of optimization or other transformations. Once typechecking is complete, simple optimizations like strength reduction and constant folding can be applied to the AST itself. Then, to generate assembly language, you can simply perform a post-order traversal of the AST and emit a few assembly instructions corresponding to each node. [1]

---

[1]This is the approach we use in a one-semester course to implement a project compiler, since there is a limited amount of time to get to the final goal of generating assembly language.

```
typedef enum {
     DAG_ASSIGN,
     DAG_DEREF,
     DAG_IADD,
     DAG_IMUL,
     ...
     DAG_NAME,
     DAG_FLOAT_VALUE,
     DAG_INTEGER_VALUE
} dag_kind_t;

struct dag_node {
     dag_kind_t kind;
     struct dag_node *left;
     struct dag_node *right;
     union {
          const char *name;
          double float_value;
          int integer_value;
     } u;
};
```

Figure 8.1: Sample DAG Data Structure Definition

However, in a production compiler, the AST isn't a great choice for an IR, mainly because the structure is *too* rich. Each node has a large number of different options and substructure: for example, an addition node could represent an integer addition, a floating point addition, a boolean-or, or a string concatenation, depending on the types of the values involved. This makes it difficult to perform robust transformations, as well as to generate an external representation. A more low-level representation is needed.

8.3   Directed Acyclic Graph

The **directed acyclic graph (DAG)** is one step simplified from the AST. A DAG is similar to the AST, except that it can have an arbitrary graph structure, and the individual nodes are greatly simplified, so that there is little or no auxiliary information beyond the type and value of each node. This requires that we have a greater number of node types, each one explicit about its purpose. For example, Figure 8.1 shows a definition of a DAG data structure that would be compatible with our project compiler.

Now suppose we compile a simple expression like x=(a+10)*(a+10).
The AST representation of this expression would directly capture the syntactic structure:

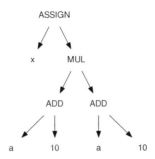

After performing typechecking, we may learn that a and b are floating point values, and therefore 10 must be converted into a float before performing floating point arithmetic. In addition, the computation a+10 need only be performed once, and the resulting value used twice.

All of that can be represented with the following DAG, which introduces a new type of node ITOF to perform integer-to-float conversion, and nodes FADD and FMUL to perform floating point arithmetic:

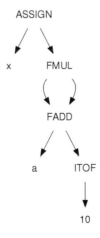

It is also common for a DAG to represent address computations related to pointers and arrays in greater detail, so that they can be shared and optimized, where possible. For example, the array lookup x=a[i] would have a very simple representation in the AST:

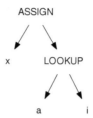

However, an array lookup is actually accomplished by adding the starting address of the array a with the index of the item i multiplied by the size of objects in the array, determined by consulting the symbol table. This could be expressed in a DAG like this:

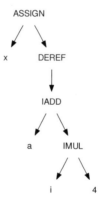

As a final step before code generation, the DAG might be expanded to include the address computations for local variables. For example, if a and i are stored on the stack at sixteen and twenty bytes past the frame pointer FP, respectively, the DAG could be expanded like this:

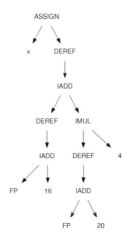

The **value-number method** can be used to construct a DAG from an AST. The idea is to build an array where each entry consists of a DAG node type, and the array index of the child nodes. Every time we wish to add a new node to the DAG, we search the array for a matching node and re-use it to avoid duplication. The DAG is constructed by performing a post-order traversal of the AST and adding each element to the array.

The DAG above could be represented by this value-number array:

#	Type	Left	Right	Value
0	NAME			x
1	NAME			a
2	INT			10
3	ITOF	2		
4	FADD	1	3	
5	FMUL	4	4	
6	ASSIGN	0	5	

Obviously, searching the table for equivalent nodes every time a new node gets added is going to have polynomial complexity. However, the absolute sizes stay relatively small, as long as each individual expression has its own DAG.

By designing the DAG representation such that all necessary information is encoded into the node type, it becomes easy to write a portable external representation. For example, we could represent each node as a symbol, followed by its children in parentheses:

```
ASSIGN(x,DEREF(IADD(DEREF(IADD(FP,16)),
                    IMUL(DEREF(IADD(FP,16)),4)))))
```

Clearly, this sort of code would not be easy for a human to read and write manually, but it is trivial to print and trivial to parse, making it easy to pass between compiler stages for analysis and optimization.

Now, what sort of optimizations might you do with the DAG? One easy optimization is **constant folding**. This is the process of reducing an expression consisting of only constants into a single value. [2] This capability is handy, because the programmer may wish to leave some expressions in an explicit form for the sake of readability or maintainability while still having the performance advantage of a single constant in the executable code.

DAG Constant Folding Algorithm
Examine a DAG recursively and collapse all operators on two constants into a single constant.

ConstantFold(DagNode n):

If n is a leaf:
    return;
Else:
    n.left = ConstantFold(n.left);
    n.right = ConstantFold(n.right);

    If n.left and n.right are constants:
        n.value = n.operator(n.left,n.right);
        n.kind = constant;
        delete n.left and n.right

---

[2]Constant folding is a narrow example of the more general technique of **partial execution** in which some parts of the program are executed at compile time, while the rest is left for runtime.

Figure 8.2: Example of Constant Folding

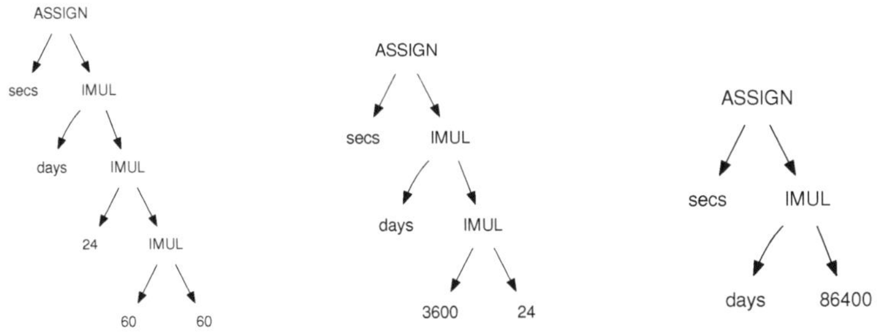

Suppose you have an expression that computes the number of seconds present in the number of days. The programmer expresses this as `secs=days*24*60*60` to make it clear that there are 24 hours in a day, 60 minutes in an hour, and 60 seconds in a minute. Figure 8.2 shows how `ConstantFold` would reduce the DAG. The algorithm descends through the tree and combines `IMUL(60,60)` into `3600`, and then `IMUL(3600,24)` into 86400.

8.4 Control Flow Graph

It is important to note that a DAG by itself is suitable for encoding expressions, but it isn't as effective for control flow or other ordered program structures. Common sub-expressions are combined under the assumption that they can be evaluated in any order (consistent with operator precedence) and the values already in the DAG do not change. This assumption does not hold when we consider multiple statements that modify values, or control flow structures that repeat or skip statements.

To reflect this, we can use a **control flow graph** to represent the higher-level structure of the program. The control flow graph is a directed graph (possibly cyclic) where each node of the graph consists of a **basic block** of sequential statements. The edges of the graph represent the possible flows of control between basic blocks. A conditional construct (like `if` or `switch`) results in branches in the graph, while a loop construct (like `for` or `while`) results in reverse edges.

For example, this bit of code:

```
for(i=0;i<10;i++) {
    if(i%2==0) {
        print "even";
    } else {
        print "odd";
    }
    print "\n";
}
return;
```

Would result in this control flow graph:

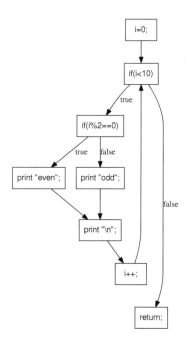

Figure 8.3: Example Control Flow Graph

Note that the control flow graph has a different structure than the AST. The AST for a for-loop would have each of the control expressions as an immediate child of the loop node, whereas the control flow graph places each one in the order it would be executed in practice. Likewise, the if statement has edges from each branch of the conditional to the following node, so that one can easily trace the flow of execution from one component to the next.

8.5 Static Single Assignment Form

The **static single assignment (SSA)** [1] form is a commonly-used representation for complex optimizations. SSA uses the information in the control flow and updates each basic block with a new restriction: *variables cannot change their values*. Instead, whenever a variable is assigned a new value, it is given a new version number.

For example, suppose that we have this bit of code:

```
int x = 1;
int a = x;
int b = a + 10;
x = 20 * b;
x = x + 30;
```

We could re-write it in SSA form like this:

```
int x_1 - 1;
int a_1 = x_1;
int b_1 = a_1 + 10;
x_2 = 20 * b_1;
x_3 = x_2 + 30;
```

A peculiarity comes when a variable is given a different value in two branches of a conditional. Following the conditional, the variable could have either value, but we don't know which one. To express this, we introduce a new function $\phi(x, y)$ which indicates that either value x or y could be selected at runtime. The ϕ function may not necessarily translate to an instruction in the assembly output, but serves to link the new value to its possible old values, reflecting the control flow graph.

For example, this code fragment:

```
if(y<10) {
    x=a;
} else {
    x=b;
}
```

Becomes this:

```
if(y_1<10) {
    x_2=a;
} else {
    x_3=b;
}
x_4 = phi(x_2,x_3);
```

8.6   Linear IR

A linear IR is an ordered sequence of instructions that is closer to the final goal of an assembly language. It loses some of the flexibility of a DAG (which does not commit to a specific ordering) but can capture expressions, statements, and control flow all within one data structure. This enables some optimization techniques that span multiple expressions.

There is no universal standard for a linear IR, but it typically looks like an idealized assembly language, with a large (or infinite) number of registers, and the typical arithmetic and control flow operations. Here, let us assume an IR where LOAD and STOR are used to move values between memory and registers, and three-address arithmetic operations read two registers and write to a third, from right to left. Our example expression would look like this:

```
1.  LOAD a           -> %r1
2.  LOAD $10         -> %r2
3.  ITOF %r2         -> %r3
4.  FADD %r1, %r3 -> %r4
5.  FMUL %r4, %r4 -> %r5
6.  STOR %r5         -> x
```

This IR is easy to store efficiently, because each instruction can be a fixed size 4-tuple representing the operation and (max) of three arguments. The external representation is also straightforward.

As the example suggests, it is most convenient to pretend that there are an infinite number of **virtual registers**, such that every new value computed writes to a new register. In this form, we can easily identify the **lifetime** of a value by observing the first point where a register is written, and the last point where a register is used. Between those two points, the value of register one must be preserved. For example, the lifetime of %r1 is from instruction 1 to instruction 4.

At any given instruction, we can also observe the set of virtual registers that are live:

```
1.  LOAD a           -> %r1      live: %r1
2.  LOAD $10         -> %r2      live: %r1 %r2
3.  ITOF %r2         -> %r3      live: %r1 %r2 %r3
4.  FADD %r1, %r3 -> %r4      live: %r1 %r3 %r4
5.  FMUL %r4, %r4 -> %r5      live: %r4 %r5
6.  STOR %r5         -> x        live: %r5
```

This observation makes it easy to perform operations related to instruction ordering. Any instruction may be moved to an earlier position (within one basic block) as long as the values it reads are not moved above their definitions. Likewise, any instruction may be moved to a later position as long as the values it writes are not moved below their uses. Moving instructions can reduce the number of physical registers needed in code generation, as well as reduce execution time in a pipelined architecture.

8.7 Stack Machine IR

An even more compact intermediate representation is a **stack machine** IR. Such a representation is designed to execute on a **virtual stack machine** that has no traditional registers, but only a stack to hold intermediate registers. A stack machine IR typically has a PUSH instruction which pushes a variable or literal value on to the stack and a POP instruction which removes an item and stores it in memory. Binary arithmetic operators (like FADD or FMUL) implicitly pop two values off the stack and push the result on the stack, while unary operators (ITOF) pop one value and push one value. A few utility instructions are needed to manipulate the stack, like a COPY instruction which pushes a duplicate value on to the stack.

To emit a stack machine IR from a DAG, we simply perform a post-order traversal of the AST and emit a PUSH for each leaf value, an arithmetic instruction for each interior node, and a POP instruction to assign a value to a variable.

Our example expression would look like this in a stack machine IR:

```
PUSH a
PUSH 10
ITOF
FADD
COPY
FMUL
POP x
```

And if executed directly, the IR would work like this:

IR Op:	PUSH a	PUSH 10	ITOF	FADD	COPY	FMUL	POP x
Stack	5.0	10	10.0	15.0	15.0	225.0	-
State:	-	5.0	-	-	15.0	-	-

A stack machine IR has many advantages. It is much more compact than a 3-tuple or 4-tuple linear representation, since there is no need to record the details of registers. It is also straightforward to implement this language in a simple interpreter.

However, a stack-based IR is slightly more difficult to translate to a conventional register-based assembly language, precisely because the explicit register names are lost. Further transformation or optimization of this form requires that we transform the implicit information dependencies in the stack-basic IR back into a more explicit form such as a DAG or a linear IR with explicit register names.

8.8 Examples

Nearly every compiler or language has its own intermediate representation with some peculiar local features. To give you a sense of what's possible, this section compares three different IRs used by compilers in 2017. For each one, we will show the output of compiling this simple arithmetic expression:

```
float f( int a, int b, float x ) {
    float y = a*x*x + b*x + 100;
    return y;
}
```

8.8.1 GIMPLE - GNU Simple Representation

The **GNU Simple Representation (GIMPLE)** is an internal IR used at the earliest stages of the GNU C compiler. GIMPLE can be thought of as a drastically simplified form of C in which all expressions have been broken down into individual operators on values in static single assignment form. Basic conditionals are allowed, and loops are implemented using `goto`.

Our simple function yields the following GIMPLE. Note that each SSA value is declared as a local variable (with a long name) and the type of each operator is still inferred from the local type declaration.

```
f (int a, int b, float x)
{
  float D.1597D.1597;
  float D.1598D.1598;
  float D.1599D.1599;
  float D.1600D.1600;
  float D.1601D.1601;
  float D.1602D.1602;
  float D.1603D.1603;
  float y;

  D.1597D.1597 = (float) a;
  D.1598D.1598 = D.1597D.1597 * x;
  D.1599D.1599 = D.1598D.1598 * x;
  D.1600D.1600 = (float) b;
  D.1601D.1601 = D.1600D.1600 * x;
  D.1602D.1602 = D.1599D.1599 + D.1601D.1601;
  y = D.1602D.1602 + 1.0e+2;
  D.1603D.1603 = y;
  return D.1603D.1603;
}
```

8.8.2 LLVM - Low Level Virtual Machine

The Low Level Virtual Machine (LLVM)[3] project is a language and a corresponding suite of tools for building optimizing compilers and interpreters. A variety of compiler front-ends support the generation of LLVM intermediate code, which can be optimized by a variety of independent tools, and then translated again into native machine code, or bytecode for virtual machines like Oracle's JVM, or Microsoft's CLR.

Our simple function yields this LLVM. Note that the first few `alloca` instructions allocate space for local variables, followed by `store` instructions that move the parameters to local variables. Then, each step of the expression is computed in SSA form and the result stored to the local variable `y`. The code is explicit at each step about the type (32-bit integer or float) and the alignment of each value.

```
define float @f(i32 %a, i32 %b, float %x) #0 {
  %1 = alloca i32, align 4
  %2 = alloca i32, align 4
  %3 = alloca float, align 4
  %y = alloca float, align 4
  store i32 %a, i32* %1, align 4
  store i32 %b, i32* %2, align 4
  store float %x, float* %3, align 4
  %4 = load i32* %1, align 4
  %5 = sitofp i32 %4 to float
  %6 = load float* %3, align 4
  %7 = fmul float %5, %6
  %8 = load float* %3, align 4
  %9 = fmul float %7, %8
  %10 = load i32* %2, align 4
  %11 = sitofp i32 %10 to float
  %12 = load float* %3, align 4
  %13 = fmul float %11, %12
  %14 = fadd float %9, %13
  %15 = fadd float %14, 1.000000e+02
  store float %15, float* %y, align 4
  %16 = load float* %y, align 4
  ret float %16
}
```

----

[3]http://llvm.org

8.8.3 *JVM - Java Virtual Machine*

The **Java Virtual Machine (JVM)** is an abstract definition of a stack-based machine. High-level code written in Java is compiled into .class files which contain a binary representation of the JVM bytecode. The earliest implementations of the JVM were interpreters which read and executed the JVM bytecode in the obvious way. Later implementations performed just-in-time (JIT) compiling of the bytecode into native assembly language, which can be executed directly.

Our simple function yields the following JVM bytecode. Note that each of the iload instructions refers to a local variable, where parameters are considered as the first few local variables. So, iload 1 pushes the first local variable (int a) on to the stack, while fload 3 pushes the third local variable (float x) on to the stack. Fixed constants are stored in an array in the class file and referenced by position, so ldc #2 pushes constant in position two (100) on to the stack.

```
 0: iload    1
 1: i2f
 2: fload    3
 4: fmul
 5: fload    3
 7: fmul
 8: iload    2
 9: i2f
10: fload    3
12: fmul
13: fadd
14: ldc      #2
16: fadd
17: fstore   4
19: fload    4
21: freturn
```

8.9   Exercises

1. Add a step to your compiler to convert the AST into a DAG by performing a post-order traversal and creating one or more DAG nodes corresponding to each AST node.

2. Write the code to export a DAG in a simple external representation as shown in this chapter. Extend the DAG suitably to represent control flow structures and function definitions.

3. Write a scanner and parser to read in the DAG external representation and reconstruct it as a data structure. Think carefully about the grammar class of the IR, and choose the simplest implementation that works.

4. Building on steps 2 and 3, write a standalone optimization tool that reads in the DAG format, performs a simple optimization like constant folding, and writes the DAG back out in the same format.

8.10   Further Reading

1. R. Cytron, J. Ferrante, B. Rosen, M. Wegman, and F. Kenneth Zadeck. "Efficiently computing static single assignment form and the control dependence graph." ACM Transactions on Programming Languages and Systems (TOPLAS) volume 13, number 4, 1991. https://doi.org/10.1145/115372.115320

2. J. Merrill, "Generic and GIMPLE: A new tree representation for entire functions." GCC Developers Summit, 2003.

3. C. Lattner and V. Adve, "LLVM: A Compilation Framework for Lifelong Program Analysis & Transformation", IEEE International Symposium on Code Generation and Optimization, 2004. https://dl.acm.org/citation.cfm?id=977673

Chapter 9 – Memory Organization

9.1 Introduction

Before digging into the translation of intermediate code to assembly language, we must discuss how the internal memory of a running program is laid out. Although a process is free to use memory in any way that it likes, a convention has developed that divides the areas of a program into logical segments, each with a different internal management strategy.

9.2 Logical Segmentation

A conventional program sees memory as a linear sequence of words, each with a numeric address starting at zero, and increasing up to some large number (e.g. 4GB on a 32-bit processor.)

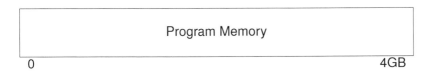

Figure 9.1: Flat Memory Model

In principle, the CPU is free to use memory in any way it sees fit. Code and data could be scattered and intermixed across memory in any order that is convenient. It is even technically possible for a CPU to modify the memory containing its code while it is running. It goes without saying that programming in this fashion would be complex, confusing, and difficult to debug.

Instead, program memory is commonly laid out by separating it into **logical segments**. Each segment is a sequential address range, dedicated to a particular purpose within the program. The segments are typically laid out in this order:

Figure 9.2: Logical Segments

- The **code segment** (also known as the **text segment**) contains the machine code of the program, corresponding to the bodies of functions in a C program.

- The **data segment** contains the global data of the program, corresponding to the global variables in a C program. The data segment may further be sub-divided into read-write data (variables) and read-only data (constants).

- The **heap segment** contains the heap, which is the area of memory that is managed dynamically at runtime by `malloc` and `free` in a C program, or `new` and `delete` in other languages. The top of the heap is historically known as the **break**.

- The **stack segment** contains the stack, which records the current execution state of the program as well as the local variables currently in use.

Typically, the heap grows "up" from lower addresses to higher addresses, while the stack grows "down" from higher to lower. In between the two segments is an invalid region of memory that is unused until overtaken by one segment or the other.

On a simple computer such as an embedded machine or microcontroller, logical segments are nothing more than an organizational convention: nothing stops the program from using memory improperly. If the heap grows too large, it can run into the stack segment (or vice versa), the program will crash (if you are lucky) or suffer silent data corruption (if you are unlucky.)

On a computer with an operating system that employs multiprogramming and memory protection, the situation is better. Each process running in the OS has its own private memory space, with the illusion of starting at address zero and extending to a high address. As a result, each process can access its own memory arbitrarily, but is prevented from accessing or modifying other processes. Within its own space, each process lays out its own code, data, heap, and stack segments.

In some operating systems, when a program is initially loaded into memory, permissions are set on each range of memory corresponding to its purpose: memory corresponding to each segment can be set appropri-

Figure 9.3: Multiprogrammed Memory Layout

ately: read-write for data, heap, and stack; read-only for constants; read-execute for code; and none for the unused area.

The permissions on the logical segments also protect a process from damaging itself in certain ways. For example, code cannot be modified at runtime because it is marked read/execute, while items on the heap cannot be executed, because they are marked read/write. (To be clear, this only prevents against accidents, not malice; a program can always ask the operating system to change the permissions on one of its own pages. For an example, look up the mprotect system call in Unix.)

If a process attempts to access memory in a prohibited way or attempts to access the unused area, a **page fault** occurs. This forces a transfer of control to the OS, which considers the process and the faulting address. If the access indicates a violation of the logical segmentation of the program, then the process is forcibly killed with the error message **segmentation fault**.[1]

Initially, a process is given a small amount of memory for the heap segment, which it manages internally to implement malloc and free. If this area is exhausted and the program still needs more, it must explicitly request it from the operating system. On traditional Unix systems, this is done with the brk system call, which requests that the heap segment be extended to a new address. If the OS agrees, then it will allocate new pages at the beginning of the invalid area, effectively extending the heap segment. If the OS does not agree, then brk will return an error code, causing malloc to return an error (indicated as a null pointer) which the program must handle.

The stack has a similar problem, in that it must be able to grow down. It is not so easy for a program to determine exactly when more stack is needed, because that happens whenever a new function is invoked, or new local variables are allocated. Instead, modern operating systems maintain a **guard page** at the top of the invalid area, adjacent to the current stack. When a process attempts to extend the stack into the invalid area, a page fault occurs, and control is transferred to the OS. If the OS sees that the faulting address is in the guard page, it can simply allocate more pages for the stack, set the page permissions appropriately, and move the guard page down to the new top of the invalid area.

Of course, there are limits on how big the heap and the stack may grow;

---

[1]And now you understand this mysterious Unix term!

every OS implements policies controlling how much memory any process or user may consume. If any of these policies are violated, the OS may decline to extend the memory of the process.

The idea of breaking a program into segments is so powerful and useful that it was common for many decades to have the concept implemented in hardware. (If you have taken a class in computer architecture and operating systems, you have probably studied this in some detail.) The basic idea is that the CPU maintains a table of segments, recording the starting address and length, along with the permissions associated with each segment. The operating system would typically set up a hardware segment to correspond to the logical organization just described.

Although hardware segmentation was widely used in operating systems through the 1980s, it has been largely replaced by paging, which was seen as simpler and more flexible. Processor vendors have responded by removing support for hardware segmentation in new designs. For example, every generation of the Intel X86 architecture from the 8086 up to the Pentium supported segmentation in 32-bit protected mode. The latest 64-bit architectures provide only paging facilities, and no segmentation. Logical segmentation continues as a useful way to organize programs in memory.

Let's continue by looking at each of the logical segments in more detail.

9.3   Heap Management

The heap contains memory that is managed dynamically at runtime. The OS does not control the internal organization of the heap, except to limit its total size. Instead, the internal structure of the heap is managed by the standard library or other runtime support software that is automatically linked into a program. In a C program, the function calls **malloc** and **free** allocate and release memory on the heap, respectively. In C++, **new** and **delete** have the same effect. Other languages manipulate the heap implicitly when objects and arrays are created and deleted.

The simplest implementation of **malloc** and **free** is to treat the entire heap as one large linked list of memory regions. Each entry in the list records the state of the region (free or in use), the size of the region, and has pointers to the previous and next regions. Here's what that might look like in C:

```c
struct chunk {
    enum { FREE, USED } state;
    int size;
    struct chunk *next;
    struct chunk *prev;
    char data[0];
};
```

(Note that we declared data as an array of length zero. This is a little trick that allows us to treat data as a variable length array, provided that the underlying memory is actually present.)

Under this scheme, the initial state of the heap is simply one entry in a linked list:

FREE	1000	data
prev	next	

Suppose that the user calls malloc(100) to allocate 100 bytes of memory. malloc will see that the (single) chunk of memory is free, but much larger than the requested size. So, it will split it into one small chunk of 100 bytes and one larger chunk with the remainder. This is accomplished by simply writing a new chunk header into the data area after 100 bytes. This is and then connect them together into a linked list:

USED	100	data	FREE	900	data
prev	next		prev	next	

Once the list has been modified, malloc returns the address of the data element within the chunk, so that the user can access it directly. It doesn't return the linked list node itself, because the user doesn't need to know about the implementation details. If there is no chunk available that is large enough to satisfy the current request, then the process must ask the OS to extend the heap by calling brk.

When the user calls free on a chunk of memory, the state of the chunk in the linked list is marked FREE, and then merged with adjacent nodes, if they are also free.

(Incidentally, now you can see why it is dangerous for a program to modify memory carelessly outside a given memory chunk. Not only could it affect other chunks, but it could damage the linked list itself, resulting in wild behavior on the next malloc or free!)

If the program always frees memory in the opposite order that it was allocated, then the heap will be nicely split into allocated and free memory. However, that isn't what happens in practice: memory can be allocated and freed in any order. Over time, the heap can degenerate into a mix of oddly sized chunks of allocated and freed memory. This is known as **memory fragmentation**.

Excessive fragmentation can result in waste: if there are many small chunks available, but none of them large enough to satisfy the current malloc, then the process has no choice but to extend the heap, leaving the small pieces unused. This increases pressure on total virtual memory consumption in the operating system.

In a language like C, memory chunks cannot be moved while in use, and so fragmentation cannot be fixed after it has already occurred. However, the memory allocator has some limited ability to avoid fragmentation by choosing the location of new allocations with care. Some simple strategies are easy to imagine and have been studied extensively:

- **Best Fit.** On each allocation, search the entire linked list and find the *smallest* free chunk that is larger than the request. This tends to leave large spaces available, but generates tiny leftover free fragments that are too small to be used.

- **Worst Fit.** On each allocation, search the entire linked list and find the *largest* free chunk that is larger than the request. Somewhat counterintuitively, this method tends to reduce fragmentation by avoiding the creation of tiny unusable fragments.

- **First Fit.** On each allocation, search the linked list from the beginning, and find the *first* fragment (large or small) that satisfies the request. This performs less work than Best Fit or Worst Fit, but performs an increasing amount of work as the linked list increases in size.

- **Next Fit.** On each allocation, search the linked list from the last examined location, and find the *next* fragment (large or small) that satisfies the request. This minimizes the amount of work done on each allocation, while distributing allocations throughout the heap.

For general purpose allocators where one cannot make assumptions about application behavior, the conventional wisdom is that Next Fit results in good performance with an acceptable level of fragmentation.

9.4   Stack Management

The **stack** is used to record the current state of the running program. Most CPUs have a specialized register – the **stack pointer** – which stores the address where the next item will be pushed or popped. Because the stack grows down from the top of memory, there is a confusing convention: pushing an item on the stack causes the stack pointer to move to a lower numbered address, while popping an item off the stack causes the stack pointer to move to a higher address. The "top" of the stack is actually at the lowest address!

Each invocation of a function occupies a range of memory in the stack, known as a **stack frame**. The stack frame contains the parameters and the local variables used by that function. When a function is called, a new stack frame is pushed; when the function returns, the stack frame is popped, and execution continues in the caller's stack frame.

Another specialized register known as the **frame pointer** (or sometimes **base pointer**) indicates the beginning of the current frame. Code within a function relies upon the frame pointer to identify the location of the current parameters and local variables.

For example, suppose that the main function calls function f, and then f calls g. If we stop the program in the middle of executing g, the stack would look like this:

Stack Frame for main:	Parameters to main	
	Old Frame Pointer	
	Local Variables	
	Return Address	
Stack Frame for f:	Parameters to f	
	Old Frame Pointer	
	Local Variables	
	Return Address	
Stack Frame for g:	Parameters to g	← Frame Pointer
	Old Frame Pointer	
	Local Variables	← Stack Pointer

↓ (stack grows down) ↓

The order and details of the elements in an stack frame differ somewhat between CPU architectures and operating systems. As long as both the caller and the callee agree on what goes in the stack frame, then any function may call another, even if they were written in different languages, or built by different compilers.

The agreement on the contents of the activation record is known as a **calling convention**. This is typically written out in a detailed technical document that is used by the designers of compilers, operating systems, and libraries to ensure that code is mutually interoperable.

There are two broad categories of calling conventions, with many opportunities for variation in between. One is to put the arguments to a function call on the stack, and the other is to place them in registers.

9.4.1 Stack Calling Convention

The conventional approach to calling a function is to push the arguments to that function on the stack (in reverse order), and then to jump to the address of the function, leaving behind a return address on the stack. Most CPUs have a specialized CALL instruction for this purpose. For example, the assembly code to call f(10,20) could be as simple as this:

```
PUSH $20
PUSH $10
CALL f
```

When f begins executing, it saves the old frame pointer currently in effect and makes space for its own local variables. As a result, the stack frame for f(10,20) looks like this:

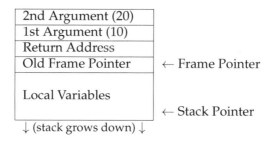

2nd Argument (20)
1st Argument (10)
Return Address
Old Frame Pointer

← Frame Pointer

Local Variables

← Stack Pointer

↓ (stack grows down) ↓

To access its arguments or local variables, f must load them from memory relative to the frame pointer. As you can see, the function arguments are found at fixed positions *above* the frame pointer, while local variables are found *below* the frame pointer. [2]

9.4.2 Register Calling Convention

An alternate approach to calling a function is to put the arguments into registers, and then call the function. For example, let us suppose that our calling convention indicates that registers %R10, %R11, etc are to be used for arguments. Under this calling convention, the assembly code to invoke f(10,20) might look like this:

```
MOVE $10 -> %R10
MOVE $20 -> %R11
CALL f
```

When f begins executing, it still must save the old frame pointer and make room for local variables. It doesn't have to load arguments from the stack; it simply expects the values in %R10 and %R11 and can compute on them right away. This could confer a significant speed advantage by avoiding memory accesses.

But, what if f is a complex function that needs to invoke other functions? It will still need to save the current values of the argument registers, in order to free them up for its own use.

To allow for this possibility, the stack frame for f must leave space for the arguments, in case they must be saved. The calling convention must define the location of the arguments, and they are typically stored *below* the return address and old frame pointer, like this:

---

[2]The arguments are pushed in reverse order in order to allow the possibility of a variable number of arguments. Argument 1 is always two words above the frame pointer, argument 2 is always three words above, and so on.

Return Address	
Old Frame Pointer	← Frame Pointer
1st Argument (10)	
2nd Argument (20)	
Local Variables	
	← Stack Pointer

↓ (stack grows down) ↓

What happens if the function has more arguments then there are registers set aside for arguments? In this case, the additional arguments are pushed on to the stack, as in the stack calling convention.

In the big picture, the choice between stack and register calling conventions doesn't matter much, except that all parties must agree on the details of the convention. The register calling convention has the slight advantage that a **leaf function** (a function that does not call other functions) can compute a simple result without accessing memory. Typically, the register calling convention is used on architectures that have a large number of registers that might otherwise go unused.

It is possible to mix the conventions in a single program, as long as both caller and callee are informed of the distinction. For example, the Microsoft X86 compilers allow keywords in function prototypes to select a convention: `cdecl` selects the stack calling convention, while `fastcall` uses registers for the first two arguments.

9.5 Locating Data

For each kind of data in a program, there must be an unambiguous method of locating that data in memory. The compiler must generate an **address computation** using the basic information available about the symbol. The computation varies with the storage class of the data:

- **Global data** has the easiest address computation. In fact, the compiler doesn't usually compute global addresses, but rather passes the *name* of each global symbol to the assembler, which then selects the address computation. In the simplest case, the assembler will generate an **absolute address** giving the exact location of the data in program memory.

  However, the simple approach isn't necessarily efficient, because an absolute address is a full word (e.g. 64 bits), the same size as an instruction in memory. This means that the assembler must use several instructions (RISC) or multi-word instructions (CISC) to load the address into a register. Assuming that most programs don't use the entire address space, it isn't usually necessary to use the entire word.

  An alternative is to use a **base-relative address** that consists of a base address given by a register plus a fixed offset given by the assembler.

For example, global data addresses could be given by a register indicating the beginning of the data segment, plus a fixed offset, while a function address could be given by a register indicating the beginning of the code segment plus a fixed offset. Such an approach can be used in dynamically loaded libraries, when the location of the library is not fixed in advance, but the location of a function within the library is known.

Yet another approach is to use a **PC-relative address** in which the exact distance in bytes between the referring instruction and the target data is computed, and then encoded into the instruction. This works as long as the relative distance is small enough (e.g. 16 bits) to fit into the address field of the instruction. This task is performed by the assembler is usually invisible to the programmer.

- **Local data** works differently. Because local variables are stored on the stack, a given local variable does not necessarily occupy the same absolute address each time it is used. If a function is called recursively, there may be multiple instances of a given local variable in use simultaneously! For this reason, local variables are always specified as an offset relative to the current frame pointer. (The offset may be positive or negative, depending on the function calling convention.) Function parameters are just a special case of local variables: a parameter's position on the stack is given precisely by its ordinal position in the parameters.

- **Heap data** can only be accessed by way of pointers that are stored as global or local variables. To access data on the heap, the compiler must generate an address computation for the pointer itself, then dereference the pointer to reach the item on the heap.

So far, we have only considered atomic data types that are easily stored in a single word of memory: booleans, integers, floats, and so forth. However, any of the more complex data types can be placed in any of the three storage classes, and require some additional handling.

An array can be stored in global, local, or heap memory, and the beginning of the array is found by one of the methods above. An element in the array is found by multiplying the index by the size of the items in the array, and adding that to the address of the array itself:

```
address(a[i]) = address(a) + sizeof(type) * i
```

The more interesting question is how to deal with the length of the array itself. In an unsafe language like C, the simple approach is to simply do nothing: if the program happens to run off the end of the array, the compiler will happily compute an address outside the array bounds, and chaos results. For some applications where performance is paramount, the simplicity of this approach trumps any increase in safety.

A safer approach is to store the length of the array at the base address of the array itself. Then, the compiler may generate code that checks the actual index against the array bounds before generating the address. This prevents any sort of runtime accident by the programmer. However, the downside is performance. Every time the programmer mentions a[i], the resulting code must contain this:

1. Compute address of array a.

2. Load length of a into a register.

3. Compare array index i to register.

4. If i is outside of array bounds, raise an exception.

5. Otherwise, compute address of a[i] and continue.

This pattern is so common that some computer architectures provide dedicated support for array bounds checking. The Intel X86 architecture, (which we will examine in detail in the next chapter) provides a unique BOUND instruction, whose only purpose is to compare a value against two array bound values, and then raise a unique "Array Bounds Exception" it it falls outside.

Structures have similar considerations. In memory, a structure is very much like an array, except that it can contain items of irregular size. To access an item within a structure, the compiler must generate an address computation of the beginning of the structure, and then add an offset corresponding to the name of item (known as the **structure tag**) within the structure. Of course, it is not necessary to perform bounds checking since the offsets are fixed at compile time.

For complex nested data structures, the address computation necessary to find an individual element can become quite complicated. For example, consider this bit of code to represent a deck of cards:

```
struct card {
    int suit;
    int rank;
};

struct deck {
    int is_shuffled;
    struct card cards[52];
};

struct deck d;

d.card[10].rank = 10;
```

To compute `d.card[10].rank`, the compiler must first generate an address computation for `d`, depending on whether it is a local or global variable. From there, the offset of `card` is added, then the offset of the tenth item, then the offset of `rank` within the card. The complete address computation is:

```
address(d.card[10].rank) =
    address(d) + offset(card) + sizeof(card)*10
                                    + offset(rank)
```

9.6 Program Loading

Before a program begins executing in memory, it first exists as a file on disk, and there must be a convention for loading it into memory. There are a variety of ways of **executable formats** for organizing a program on disk, ranging from very simple to very complex. Here are a few examples to give you the idea.

The simplest computer systems simply store an executable as a **binary blob** on disk. The program code, data, and initial state of the heap and stack are simply dumped into one file without distinction. To run the program, the OS must simply load the contents of the file into memory, and then jump to the first location of the program to begin execution.

This approach is about as simple as one can imagine. It does work, but it has several limitations. One is that the format wastes space on uninitialized data. For example, if the program declares a large global array where each element has the value zero, then every single zero in that array will be stored in the file. Another is that the OS has no insight into how the program intends to use memory, so it is unable to set permissions on each logical segment, as discussed above. Yet another is that the binary blob has no identifying information to show that it is an executable.

However, the binary blob approach is still occasionally used in places where programs are small and simplicity is paramount. For example, the very first boot stage of PC operating system reads in a single sector from the boot hard disk containing a binary blob, which then carries out the second stage of booting. Embedded systems often have very small programs measured in a few kilobytes, and rely on binary blobs.

An improved approach used in classic Unix systems for many years is the **a.out** executable format. [3] There are many slight variations on the format, but they all share the same basic structure. The executable file consists of a short header structure, followed by the text, initialized data, and symbol table:

Header	Text	Data	Symbols

---

[3]The first Unix assembler sent its output to a file named `a.out` by default. In the absence of any other name for the format, the name stuck.

The header structure itself is just a few bytes that allow the operating system to interpret the rest of the file:

Magic Number
Text Section Size
Data Section Size
BSS Size
Symbol Table Size
Entry Point

The **magic number** is a unique integer that clearly defines the file as an executable: if the file does not begin with this magic number, the OS will not even attempt to execute it. Different magic numbers are defined for executables, unlinked object files, and shared libraries. The **text size** field indicates the number of bytes in the text section that follows the header. The **data size** field indicates the amount of *initialized* data that appears in the file, while the **BSS size** field indicates the amount of *uninitialized data*. [4]

The uninitialized data need not be stored in the file. Instead it is simply allocated in memory as part of the data segment when the program is loaded. The **symbol table** in the executable lists each of the variable and function names used in the program along with their locations in the code and data segment; this permits a debugger to interpret the meaning of addresses. Finally, the **entry point** gives the address of the starting point of the program (typically `main`) in the text segment. This allows the starting point to be something other than the first address in the program.

The `a.out` format is a big improvement over a binary blob, and is still supported and usable today in many operating systems. However, it isn't quite powerful enough to support many of the features needed by modern languages, particularly dynamically loaded libraries.

The **Extensible Linking Format (ELF)** is widely used today across many operating systems to represent executables, object files, and shared libraries. Like `a.out`, an ELF file has multiple sections representing code, data, and bss, but it can have an arbitrary number of additional sections for debugging data, initialization and finalization code, metadata about the tools used, and so forth. The number of *sections* in the file outnumbers the *segments* in memory, and so a **section table** in the ELF file indicates how multiple sections are to be mapped into a single segment.

---

[4]BSS stands for "Block Started by Symbol" and first appeared in an assembler for IBM 704 in the 1950s.

File Header
Program Header
Code Section
Data Section
Read-Only Section
. . .
Section Header

9.7 Further Reading

1. Remzi Arpaci-Dusseau and Andrea Arpaci-Dusseau, "Operating Systems: Three Easy Pieces", Arpaci-Dusseau Books, 2015.
   `http://www.ostep.org`
   Operating systems is usually the course in which memory management is covered in great detail. If you need a refresher on memory allocators (or anything else in operating systems), check out this online textbook.

2. John R. Levine, "Linkers and Loaders", Morgan Kaufmann, 1999.
   This book provides a detailed look at linkers and loaders, which is an often-overlooked topic that falls in cracks between compilers and operating systems. A solid understanding of linking is necessarily to create and use libraries effectively.

3. Paul R. Wilson, "Uniprocessor Garbage Collection Techniques", Lecture Notes in Computer Science, volume 637, 1992.
   `https://link.springer.com/chapter/10.1007/BFb0017182`
   This widely-read article gives an accessible overview of the key techniques of garbage collection, which are an essential component of the runtime of modern dynamic languages.

Chapter 10 – Assembly Language

10.1 Introduction

In order to build a compiler, you must have a working knowledge of at least one kind of assembly language. And, it helps to see two or more variations of assembly, so as to fully appreciate the distinctions between architectures. Some of these differences, such as register structure, are quite fundamental, while some of the differences are merely superficial.

We have observed that many students seem to think that assembly language is rather obscure and complicated. Well, it is true that the complete manual for a CPU is extraordinarily thick, and may document hundreds of instructions and obscure addressing modes. However, it's been our experience that it is really only necessary to learn a small subset of a given assembly language (perhaps 30 instructions) in order to write a functional compiler. Many of the additional instructions and features exist to handle special cases for operating systems, floating point math, and multi-media computing. You can do almost everything needed with the basic subset.

We will look at two different CPU architectures that are in wide use today: X86 and ARM. The Intel X86 is a CISC architecture that has evolved since the 1970s from 8-bit to 64-bit and is now the dominant chip in personal computers, laptops, and high performance servers. The ARM processor is a RISC architecture began life as a 32-bit chip for the personal computer market, and is now the dominant chip for low-power and embedded devices such as mobile phones and tablets.

This chapter will give you a working knowledge of the basics of each architecture, but you will need a good reference to look up more details. We recommend that you consult the Intel Software Developer Manual [1] and the ARM Architecture Reference Manual [3] for the complete details. (Note that each section is meant to be parallel and self-contained, so some explanatory material is repeated for both X86 and ARM.)

10.2   Open Source Assembler Tools

A given assembly language can have multiple dialects for the same CPU, depending on whether one uses the assembler provided by the chip vendor, or other open source tools. For consistency, we will give examples in the assembly dialect supported by the GNU compiler and assembler, which are known as gcc and as (or sometimes gas.)

A good way to get started is to view the assembler output of the compiler for a C program. To do this, run gcc with the -S flag, and the compiler will produce assembly output rather than a binary program. On Unix-like systems, assembly code is stored in files ending with .s, which indicates "source" file.

If you run gcc -S hello.c -o hello.s on this C program:

```
#include <stdio.h>

int main( int argc, char *argv[] )
{
    printf("hello %s\n","world");
    return 0;
}
```

then you should see output similar to this in hello.s

```
.file    "test.c"
.data
.LC0:
        .string "hello %s\n"
.LC1:
        .string "world"
.text
.globl main
main:
        PUSHQ   %rbp
        MOVQ    %rsp, %rbp
        SUBQ    $16, %rsp
        MOVQ    %rdi, -8(%rbp)
        MOVQ    %rsi, -16(%rbp)
        MOVQ    $.LC0, %rax
        MOVQ    $.LC1, %rsi
        MOVQ    %rax, %rdi
        MOVQ    $0, %rax
        CALL    printf
        MOVQ    $0, %rax
        LEAVE
        RET
```

(There are many valid ways to compile `hello.c` and so the output of your compiler may be somewhat different.)

Regardless of the CPU architecture, the assembly code has three different kinds of elements:

Directives begin with a dot and indicate structural information useful to the assembler, linker, or debugger, but are not in and of themselves assembly instructions. For example, `.file` simply records the name of the original source file to assist the debugger. `.data` indicates the start of the data segment of the program, while `.text` indicates the start of the program segment. `.string` indicates a string constant within the data section, and `.globl main` indicates that the label `main` is a global symbol that can be accessed by other code modules.

Labels end with a colon and indicate by their position the association between names and locations. For example, the label `.LC0:` indicates that the immediately following string should be called `.LC0`. The label `main:` indicates that the instruction `PUSHQ %rbp` is the first instruction of the main function. By convention, labels beginning with a dot are temporary local labels generated by the compiler, while other symbols are user-visible functions and global variables. The labels do not become part of the resulting machine code *per se*, but they are present in the resulting object code for the purposes of linking, and in the eventual executable, for purposes of debugging.

Instructions are the actual assembly code like (`PUSHQ %rbp`), typically indented to visually distinguish them from directives and labels. Instructions in GNU assembly are not case sensitive, but we will generally uppercase them, for consistency.

To take this `hello.s` and turn it into a runnable program, just run `gcc`, which will figure out that it is an assembly program, assemble it, and link it with the standard library:

```
% gcc hello.s -o hello
% ./hello
hello world
```

It is also interesting to compile the assembly code into object code, and then use the `nm` utility to display the symbols ("names") present in the code:

```
% gcc hello.s -c -o hello.o
% nm hello.o
0000000000000000 T main
                 U printf
```

This display the information available to the linker. `main` is present in the text (`T`) section of the object, at location zero, and `printf` is undefined

(U), since it must be obtained from the standard library. But none of the labels like `.LC0` appear because they were not declared as `.globl`.

As you are learning assembly language, take advantage of an existing compiler: write some simple functions to see what `gcc` generates. This can give you some starting points to identify new instructions and techniques to use.

10.3   X86 Assembly Language

X86 is a generic term that refers to the series of microprocessors descended from (or compatible with) the Intel 8088 processor used in the original IBM PC, including the 8086, 80286, '386, '486, and many others. Each generation of CPUs added new instructions and addressing modes from 8-bit to 16-bit to 32-bit, all while retaining backwards compatibility with old code. A variety of competitors (such as AMD) produced compatible chips that implemented the same instruction set.

However, Intel broke with tradition in the 64-bit generation by introducing a new brand (Itanium) and architecture (IA64) that was *not* backwards compatible with old code. Instead, it implemented a new concept known as Very Long Instruction Word (VLIW) in which multiple concurrent operations were encoded into a single word. This had the potential for significant speedups due to instruction-level parallelism but represented a break with the past.

AMD stuck with the old ways and produced a 64-bit architecture (AMD64) that *was* backwards compatible with both Intel and AMD chips. While the technical merits of both approaches were debatable, the AMD approach won in the marketplace, and Intel followed by producing its own 64-bit architecture (Intel64) that was compatible with AMD64 and its own previous generation of chips. X86-64 is the generic name that covers both AMD64 and Intel64 architectures.

X86-64 is a fine example of CISC (complex instruction set computing). There are a very large number of instructions with many different submodes, some of them designed for very narrow tasks. However, a small subset of instructions will let us accomplish a lot.

10.3.1   Registers and Data Types

X86-64 has sixteen (almost) general purpose 64-bit integer registers:

%rax	%rbx	%rcx	%rdx	%rsi	%rdi	%rbp	%rsp
%r8	%r9	%r10	%r11	%r12	%r13	%r14	%r15

These registers are *almost* general purpose because earlier versions of the processors intended for each register to be used for a specific purpose, and not all instructions could be applied to every register. The names of

A Note on AT&T Syntax versus Intel Syntax

Note that the GNU tools use the traditional AT&T syntax, which is used across many processors on Unix-like operating systems, as opposed to the Intel syntax typically used on DOS and Windows systems. The following instruction is given in AT&T syntax:

```
MOVQ %RSP, %RBP
```

MOVQ is the name of the instruction, and the percent signs indicate that RSP and RBP are registers. In the AT&T syntax, the source is always given first, and the destination is always given second.

In other places (such as the Intel manual), you will see the Intel syntax, which (among other things) dispenses with the percent signs and *reverses* the order of the arguments. For example, this is the same instruction in the Intel syntax:

```
MOVQ RBP, RSP
```

When reading manuals and web pages, be careful to determine whether you are looking at AT&T or Intel syntax: look for the percent signs!

the lower eight registers indicate the purpose for which each was originally intended: for example, %rax is the accumulator.

As the design developed, new instructions and addressing modes were added to make the various registers almost equal. A few remaining instructions, particularly related to string processing, require the use of %rsi and %rdi. In addition, two registers are reserved for use as the stack pointer (%rsp) and the base pointer (%rbp). The final eight registers are numbered and have no specific restrictions.

The architecture has expanded from 8 to 64 bits over the years, and so each register has some internal structure. The lowest 8 bits of the %rax register are an 8-bit register %al, and the next 8 bits are known as %ah. The low 16 bits are collectively known as %ax, the low 32-bits as %eax, and the whole 64 bits as %rax.

Figure 10.1: X86 Register Structure

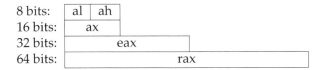

The numbered registers %r8-%r15 have the same structure, but a slightly different naming scheme:

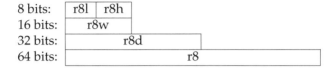

Figure 10.2: X86 Register Structure

To keep things simple, we will focus our attention on the 64-bit registers. However, most production compilers use a mix of modes: a byte can represent a boolean; a longword is usually sufficient for integer arithmetic, since most programs don't need integer values above 2^{32}; and a quadword is needed to represent a memory address, enabling up to 16EB (exa-bytes) of virtual memory.

10.3.2   Addressing Modes

The MOV instruction moves data between registers and to and from memory in a variety of different modes. A single letter suffix determines the size of data to be moved:

Suffix	Name	Size	
B	BYTE	1 byte	(8 bits)
W	WORD	2 bytes	(16 bits)
L	LONG	4 bytes	(32 bits)
Q	QUADWORD	8 bytes	(64 bits)

MOVB moves a byte, MOVW moves a word, MOVL moves a long, MOVQ moves a quad-word.[1] Generally, the size of the locations you are moving to and from must match the suffix. In some cases, you can leave off the suffix, and the assembler will infer the right size. However, this can have unexpected consequences, so we will make a habit of using the suffix.

The arguments to MOV can have one of several addressing modes.

- A **global value** is simply referred to by an unadorned name such as x or printf, which the assembler translates into an absolute address or an address computation.

- An **immediate value** is a constant value indicated by a dollar sign such as $56, and has a limited range, depending on the instruction in use.

- A **register value** is the name of a register such as %rbx.

---

[1]Careful: These terms are not portable. A *word* has a different size on different machines.

- An **indirect value** refers to a value by the address contained in a register. For example, (%rsp) refers to the value pointed to by %rsp.

- A **base-relative** value is given by adding a constant to the name of a register. For example, −16(%rcx) refers to the value at the memory location sixteen bytes below the address indicated by %rcx. This mode is important for manipulating stacks, local values, and function parameters, where the start of an object is given by a register.

- A **complex** address is of the form $D(R_A, R_B, C)$ which refers to the value at address $R_A + R_B * C + D$. Both R_A and R_B are general purpose registers, while C can have the value 1, 2, 4, or 8, and D can be any integer displacement. This mode is used to select an item within an array, where R_A gives the base of the array, R_B gives the index into the array, C gives the size of the items in the array, and D is an offset relative to that item.

Here is an example of using each kind of addressing mode to load a 64-bit value into %rax:

Mode	Example
Global Symbol	MOVQ x, %rax
Immediate	MOVQ $56, %rax
Register	MOVQ %rbx, %rax
Indirect	MOVQ (%rsp), %rax
Base-Relative	MOVQ −8(%rbp), %rax
Complex	MOVQ −16(%rbx,%rcx,8), %rax

For the most part, the same addressing modes may be used to store data into registers and memory locations. There are some exceptions. For example, it is not possible to use base-relative for both arguments of MOV: MOVQ −8(%rbx), −8(%rbx). To see exactly what combinations of addressing modes are supported, you must read the manual pages for the instruction in question.

In some cases, you may want to load the *address* of a variable instead of its value. This is handy when working with strings or arrays. For this purpose, use the LEA (load effective address) instruction, which can perform the same address computations as MOV:

Mode	Example
Global Symbol	LEAQ x, %rax
Base-Relative	LEAQ −8(%rbp), %rax
Complex	LEAQ −16(%rbx,%rcx,8), %rax

10.3.3 Basic Arithmetic

You will need four basic arithmetic instructions for your compiler: integer addition, subtraction, multiplication, and division.

ADD and SUB have two operands: a source and a destructive target. For example, this instruction:

```
ADDQ %rbx, %rax
```

adds %rbx to %rax, and places the result in %rax, overwriting what might have been there before. This requires a little care, so that you don't accidentally clobber a value that you might want to use later. For example, you could translate `c = a+b+b;` like this:

```
MOVQ a, %rax
MOVQ b, %rbx
ADDQ %rbx, %rax
ADDQ %rbx, %rax
MOVQ %rax, c
```

The `IMUL` instruction is a little unusual, because multiplying two 64-bit integers results in a 128-bit integer, in the general case. `IMUL` takes its argument, multiplies it by the contents of %rax, and then places the low 64 bits of the result in %rax and the high 64 bits in %rdx. (This is implicit: %rdx is not mentioned in the instruction.)

For example, suppose that you wish to translate `c = b*(b+a);`, where a, and b, and c are global integers. Here is one possible translation:

```
MOVQ   a, %rax
MOVQ   b, %rbx
ADDQ   %rbx, %rax
IMULQ  %rbx
MOVQ   %rax, c
```

The IDIV instruction does the same thing, except backwards: it starts with a 128 bit integer value whose low 64 bits are in %rax and high 64 bits in %rdx, and divides it by the value given in the instruction. The quotient is placed in %rax and the remainder in %rdx. (If you want to implement the modulus instruction instead of division, just use the value of %rdx.)

To set up a division, you must make sure that both registers have the necessary sign-extended value. If the dividend fits in the lower 64 bits, but is negative, then the upper 64 bits must all be ones to complete the twos-complement representation. The CQO instruction serves the very specific purpose of sign-extending %rax into %rdx for divsion.

For example, to divide a by five:

```
MOVQ a,  %rax     # set the low 64 bits of the dividend
CQO               # sign-extend %rax into %rdx
IDIVQ $5          # divide %rdx:%rax by 5,
                  #           leaving result in %rax
```

The instructions INC and DEC increment and decrement a register de-
structively. For example, the statement a = ++b could be translated as:

```
MOVQ b, %rax
INCQ %rax
MOVQ %rax,b
MOVQ %rax, a
```

The instructions AND, OR, and XOR perform destructive *bitwise* boolean
operations on two values. Bitwise means that the operation is applied to
each individual bit in the operands, and stored in the result.
So, AND $0101B $0110B would yield the result $0100B. In a similar
way, the NOT instruction inverts each bit in the operand. For example,
the bitwise C expression c = (a & ~b); could be translated like this:

```
MOVQ a, %rax
MOVQ b, %rbx
NOTQ %rbx
ANDQ %rax, %rbx
MOVQ %rbx, c
```

Be careful here: these instructions *do not* implement logical boolean operations according to the C representation that you are probably familiar
with. For example, if you define "false" to be the integer zero, and true
to be any non-zero value. In that case, $0001 is true, but NOT $0001B is
$1110B, which is also true! To implement that correctly, you need to use
CMP with conditionals described below.[2]

Like the MOV instruction, the various arithmetic instructions can work
on a variety of addressing modes. However, for your compiler project, you
will likely find it most convenient to use MOV to load values in and out of
registers, and then use only registers to perform arithmetic.

---

[2] Alternatively, you could could use the bitwise operators as logical operators if you give
true the integer value -1 (all ones) and false the integer value zero.

10.3.4 Comparisons and Jumps

Using the JMP instruction, we may create a simple infinite loop that counts up from zero using the %rax register:

```
      MOVQ $0, %rax
loop: INCQ %rax
      JMP loop
```

To define more useful structures such as terminating loops and if-then statements, we must have a mechanism for evaluating values and changing program flow. In most assembly languages, these are handled by two different kinds of instructions: compares and jumps.

All comparisons are done with the CMP instruction. CMP compares two different registers and then sets a few bits in the internal EFLAGS register, recording whether the values are the same, greater, or lesser. You don't need to look at the EFLAGS register directly. Instead a selection of conditional jumps examine the EFLAGS register and jump appropriately:

Instruction	Meaning
JE	Jump if Equal
JNE	Jump if Not Equal
JL	Jump if Less
JLE	Jump if Less or Equal
JG	Jump if Greater
JGE	Jump if Greater or Equal

For example, here is a loop to count %rax from zero to five:

```
        MOVQ $0, %rax
loop:   INCQ %rax
        CMPQ $5, %rax
        JLE  loop
```

And here is a conditional assignment: if global variable x is greater than zero, then global variable y gets ten, else twenty:

```
        MOVQ x, %rax
        CMPQ $0, %rax
        JLE  .L1
.L0:
        MOVQ $10, $rbx
        JMP  .L2
.L1:
        MOVQ $20, $rbx
.L2:
        MOVQ %rbx, y
```

Note that jumps require the compiler to define target labels. These labels must be unique and private within one assembly file, but cannot be seen outside the file unless a `.globl` directive is given. Labels like `.L0`, `.L1`, etc, can be generated by the compiler on demand.

10.3.5   The Stack

The stack is an auxiliary data structure used primarily to record the function call history of the program along with local variables that do not fit in registers. By convention, the stack grows *downward* from high values to low values. The %rsp register is known as the **stack pointer** and keeps track of the bottom-most item on the stack.

To push %rax onto the stack, we must subtract 8 (the size of %rax in bytes) from %rsp and then write to the location pointed to by %rsp:

```
SUBQ $8, %rsp
MOVQ %rax, (%rsp)
```

Popping a value from the stack involves the opposite:

```
MOVQ (%rsp), %rax
ADDQ $8, %rsp
```

To discard the most recent value from the stack, just move the stack pointer the appropriate number of bytes :

```
ADDQ $8, %rsp
```

Of course, pushing to and popping from the stack referred to by %rsp is so common, that the two operations have their own instructions that behave exactly as above:

```
PUSHQ %rax
POPQ  %rax
```

Note that, in 64-bit code, `PUSH` and `POP` are limited to working with 64-bit values, so a manual `MOV` and `ADD` must be used if it is necessary to move smaller items to/from the stack.

10.3.6   Calling a Function

Prior to the 64-bit architecture described here, a simple stack calling convention was used: arguments were pushed on the stack in reverse order, then the function was invoked with CALL. The called function looked for the arguments on the stack, did its work, and returned the result in %eax. The caller then removed the arguments from the stack.

However, 64-bit code uses a register calling convention, in order to exploit the larger number of available registers in the X86-64 architecture. [3] This convention is known as the **System V ABI** [2] and is written out in a lengthy technical document. The complete convention is quite complicated, but this summary handles the basic cases:

Figure 10.3: Summary of System V ABI Calling Convention

- The first six integer arguments (including pointers and other types that can be stored as integers) are placed in the registers %rdi, %rsi, %rdx, %rcx, %r8, and %r9, in that order.

- The first eight floating point arguments are placed in the registers %xmm0-%xmm7, in that order.

- Arguments in excess of those registers are pushed onto the stack.

- If the function takes a variable number of arguments (like printf) then the %rax register must be set to the number of floating point arguments.

- The return value of the function is placed in %rax.

In addition, we also need to know how the remaining registers are handled. A few are **caller saved**, meaning that the calling function must save those values before invoking another function. Others are **callee saved**, meaning that a function, when called, must save the values of those registers, and restore them on return. The argument and result registers need not be saved at all. Figure 10.4 shows these requirements.

To invoke a function, we must first compute the arguments and place them in the desired registers. Then, we must push the two caller-saved registers (%r10 and %r11) on the stack, to save their values. We then issue the CALL instruction, which pushes the current instruction pointer on to the stack then jumps to the code location of the function. Upon return from the function, we pop the two caller-saved registers off of the stack, and look for the return value of the function in the %rax register.

---

[3]Note that there is nothing *stopping* you from writing a compiler that uses a stack calling convention. But if you want to invoke functions compiled by others (like the standard library) then you need to stick to the convention already in use.

Here is an example. The following C program:

```
int x=0;
int y=10;

int main()
{
    x = printf("value: %d",y);
}
```

could be translated to this:

```
.data
x:
        .quad 0
y:
        .quad 10
str:
        .string "value: %d\n"

.text
.globl main
main:
        MOVQ  $str, %rdi  # first argument in %rdi: string
        MOVQ  y,    %rsi  # second argument in %rsi: y
        MOVQ  $0,   %rax  # there are zero float args

        PUSHQ %r10        # save the caller-saved regs
        PUSHQ %r11

        CALL  printf      # invoke printf

        POPQ  %r11        # restore the caller-saved regs
        POPQ  %r10

        MOVQ  %rax, x     # save the result in x

        RET               # return from main function
```

Figure 10.4: System V ABI Register Assignments

Register	Purpose	Who Saves?
%rax	result	not saved
%rbx	scratch	callee saves
%rcx	argument 4	not saved
%rdx	argument 3	not saved
%rsi	argument 2	not saved
%rdi	argument 1	not saved
%rbp	base pointer	callee saves
%rsp	stack pointer	callee saves
%r8	argument 5	not saved
%r9	argument 6	not saved
%r10	scratch	CALLER saves
%r11	scratch	CALLER saves
%r12	scratch	callee saves
%r13	scratch	callee saves
%r14	scratch	callee saves
%r15	scratch	callee saves

10.3.7 Defining a Leaf Function

Because function arguments are passed in registers, it is easy to write a **leaf function** that computes a value without calling any other functions. For example, code for the following function:

```
square: function integer ( x: integer ) =
{
    return x*x;
}
```

Could be as simple as this:

```
.global square
square:
    MOVQ  %rdi, %rax  # copy first argument to %rax
    IMULQ %rax        # multiply it by itself
                      # result is already in %rax
    RET               # return to caller
```

Unfortunately, this won't work for a function that wants to invoke other functions, because we haven't set up the stack properly. A more complex approach is needed for the general case.

10.3.8 Defining a Complex Function

A complex function must be able to invoke other functions and compute expressions of arbitrary complexity, and then return to the caller with the original state intact. Consider the following recipe for a function that accepts three arguments and uses two local variables:

```
.globl func
func:
    pushq %rbp              # save the base pointer
    movq  %rsp, %rbp        # set new base pointer

    pushq %rdi             # save first argument on the stack
    pushq %rsi             # save second argument on the stack
    pushq %rdx             # save third argument on the stack

    subq  $16, %rsp        # allocate two more local variables

    pushq %rbx             # save callee-saved registers
    pushq %r12
    pushq %r13
    pushq %r14
    pushq %r15

    ### body of function goes here ###

    popq %r15              # restore callee-saved registers
    popq %r14
    popq %r13
    popq %r12
    popq %rbx

    movq  %rbp, %rsp       # reset stack pointer
    popq  %rbp             # recover previous base pointer
    ret                    # return to the caller
```

There is a lot to keep track of here: the arguments given to the function, the information necessary to return, and space for local computations. For this purpose, we use the base register pointer %rbp. Whereas the stack pointer %rsp points to the end of the stack where new data will be pushed, the base pointer %rbp points to the start of the values used by this function. The space between %rbp and %rsp is known as the **stack frame** for this function call.

There is one more complication: each function needs to use a selection of registers to perform computations. However, what happens when one function is called in the middle of another? We do not want any registers currently in use by the caller to be clobbered by the called function. To prevent this, each function must save and restore all of the registers that it uses by pushing them onto the stack at the beginning, and popping them off of the stack before returning. According to Figure 10.4, each function must preserve the values of %rsp, %rbp, %rbx, and %r12-%r15 when it completes.

Here is the stack layout for func, defined above:

Contents	Address	
old %rip register	8(%rbp)	
old %rbp register	(%rbp)	← %rbp points here
argument 0	-8(%rbp)	
argument 1	-16(%rbp)	
argument 2	-24(%rbp)	
local variable 0	-32(%rbp)	
local variable 1	-40(%rbp)	
saved register %rbx	-48(%rbp)	
saved register %r12	-56(%rbp)	
saved register %r13	-64(%rbp)	
saved register %r14	-72(%rbp)	
saved register %r15	-80(%rbp)	← %rsp points here

Figure 10.5: Example X86-64 Stack Layout

Note that the base pointer (%rbp) locates the start of the stack frame. So, within the body of the function, we may use base-relative addressing against the base pointer to refer to both arguments and locals. The arguments to the function follow the base pointer, so argument zero is at -8(%rbp), argument one at -16(%rbp), and so forth. Past those are local variables to the function at -32(%rbp) and then saved registers at -48(%rbp). The stack pointer points to the last item on the stack. If we use the stack for additional purposes, data will be pushed to further negative values. (Note that we have assumed all arguments and variables are 8 bytes large: different types would result in different offsets.)

Here is a complete example that puts it all together. Suppose that you have a C-minor function defined as follows:

```
compute: function integer
         ( a: integer, b: integer, c: integer )
{
    int x, y;
    x = a+b+c;
    y = x*5;
    return y;
}
```

A complete translation of the function is on the next page. The code given is correct, but rather conservative. As it turned out, this particular function didn't need to use registers `%rbx-%r15`, so it wasn't necessary to save and restore them. In a similar way, we could have kept the arguments in registers without saving them to the stack. The result could have been computed directly into `%rax` rather than saving it to a local variable. These optimizations are easy to make when writing code by hand, but not so easy when writing a compiler.

For your first attempt at building a compiler, your code created will (probably) not be very efficient if each statement is translated independently. The preamble to a function must save all the registers, because it does not know *a priori* which registers will be used later. Likewise, a statement that computes a value must save it back to a local variable, because it does not know beforehand whether the local will be used as a return value. We will explore these issues later in Chapter 12 on optimization.

Figure 10.6: Complete X86 Example

```
.globl compute
compute:
##################### preamble of function sets up stack
pushq %rbp              # save the base pointer
movq  %rsp, %rbp        # set new base pointer to rsp

pushq %rdi              # save first argument (a) on the stack
pushq %rsi              # save second argument (b) on the stack
pushq %rdx              # save third argument (c) on the stack

subq  $16, %rsp         # allocate two more local variables

pushq %rbx              # save callee-saved registers
pushq %r12
pushq %r13
pushq %r14
pushq %r15

###################### body of function starts here
movq  -8(%rbp),  %rbx   # load each arg into a register
movq  -16(%rbp), %rcx
movq  -24(%rbp), %rdx

addq  %rdx, %rcx        # add the args together
addq  %rcx, %rbx
movq  %rbx, -32(%rbp)   # store the result into local 0 (x)

movq  -32(%rbp), %rbx   # load local 0 (x) into a register.
movq  $5, %rcx          # load 5 into a register
movq  %rbx, %rax        # move argument in rax
imulq %rcx              # multiply them together
movq  %rax, -40(%rbp)   # store the result in local 1 (y)

movq  -40(%rbp), %rax   # move local 1 (y) into the result

#################### epilogue of function restores the stack
popq  %r15              # restore callee-saved registers
popq  %r14
popq  %r13
popq  %r12
popq  %rbx

movq  %rbp, %rsp        # reset stack to base pointer.
popq  %rbp              # restore the old base pointer

ret                     # return to caller
```

10.4 ARM Assembly

The ARM processor architecture has a history almost as long as the X86 architecture. It originated as the 32-bit **Acorn RISC Machine** used in the **Acorn Archimedes** personal computer in 1987, and has since evolved into a wide-used low-power CPU employed in many embedded and mobile systems, now known as the **Advanced RISC Machine (ARM)**. The evolving architecture has been implemented by a number of chip vendors working from a common architecture definition. The most recent versions of the architecture are ARMv7-A (32-bit) and ARMv8-A (64-bit.) This chapter will focus on the 32-bit architecture, with some remarks on differences in the 64-bit architecture at the end.

ARM is an example of a **Reduced Instruction Set Computer (RISC)** rather than a **Complex Instruction Set Computer (CISC)**. Compared to X86, ARM relies on a smaller set of instructions which are simpler to pipeline or run in parallel, reducing the complexity and energy consumption of the chip. ARM is sometimes considered "partially" RISC due to a few exceptions. For example, the difference in the time to execute some ARM instruction makes the pipeline imperfect, the inclusion of a barrel shifter for preprocessing brings forward more complex instructions, and conditional execution decreases some of the potential instructions executed and lead to less branching instructions so less energy used by the processor. We will mainly be focusing on the elements of the instruction set which allow us to do the most in a compiler, leaving the more complex aspects and optimizations of the programming language for later.

10.4.1 Registers and Data Types

ARM-32 has a set of 16 general purpose registers, r0-r15, with the following conventions for use:

Name	Alias	Purpose
r0		General Purpose Register
r1		General Purpose Register
...		. . .
r10		General Purpose Register
r11	fp	Frame Pointer
r12	ip	Intra Procedure Call Scratch Register
r13	sp	Stack Pointer
r14	lr	Link Register (Return Address)
r15	pc	Program Counter

In addition to general purpose registers, there are two registers that cannot be directly accessed: the Current Program Status Register (CPSR) and the Saved Program Status Register (SPSR). These hold the results of comparison operations, as well as privileged data regarding the process state. A user-level program cannot access these directly, but they can be set as a side effect of some operations.

ARM uses the following suffixes to indicate data sizes. Note that these have *different* meanings than in X86 assembly! If no suffix is given, the assembler assumes an unsigned word operand. Signed types are used to provide appropriate sign-extension when loading a small data type into a larger register. There is no register naming structure for anything below a word.

Data Type	Suffix	Size
Byte	B	8 bits
Halfword	H	16 bits
Word	W	32 bits
Double Word	-	64 bits
Signed Byte	SB	8 bits
Signed Halfword	SH	16 bits
Signed Word	SW	32 bits
Double Word	-	64 bits

10.4.2 Addressing Modes

ARM makes the use of two different classes of instructions to move data between registers and between registers and memeory. MOV copies data and constants between registers, while LDR (load) and STR (store) instructions are used to move data between registers and memory.

The MOV instruction is used to move a known immediate value into a given register or move another register into the first register. In ARM, immediate values are denoted by a #. However, these immediate values must be 16-bits or less. If they are greater, the LDR instruction must be used instead. Most ARM instructions indicate the destination register on the left and the source register on the left. (STR is an exception.) So for moving data between immediate values and registers we would have the following:

Mode	Example
Immediate	MOV r0, #3
Register	MOV r1, r0

The mnemonic letter for each data type can be appended to the MOV instruction allowing us to be sure of which is being transferred and how that data is being transferred. If not, the assembler assumes an entire word.

To move values in and out of memory, use the Load (LDR) and Store (STR) instructions, both of which indicate the source or destination register as the first argument, and the source or destination memory address as the second argument. In the simplest case, the address is given by a register and indicated in brackets:

Figure 10.7: ARM Addressing Modes

Address Mode	Example
Literal	LDR Rd, =0xABCD1234
Absolute Address	LDR Rd, =label
Register Indirect	LDR Rd, [Ra]
Preindexing - Immediate	LDR Rd, [Ra, #4]
Preindexing - Register	LDR Rd, [Ra, Ro]
Preindexing - Immediate & Writeback	LDR Rd, [Ra, #4]!
Preindexing - Register & Writeback	LDR Rd, [Ra, Ro]!
Postindexing - Immediate	LDR Rd, [Ra], #4
Postindexing - Register	LDR Rd, [Ra], Ro

```
LDR Rd, [Ra]
STR Rs, [Ra]
```

In this case, Rd denotes the destination register, Rs denotes the source register and Ra denotes the register containing the address. (Note that the memory address must be aligned to the data type: a byte can load a value from any address, a half-word from every even address, and so on.)

Both LDR and STR support a variety of addressing modes, shown in Figure 10.7. First, LDR can be used to load a literal value (or label address) of a full 32-bits into a register. (See the next section for a full explanation of this.) Unlike X86, there is no single instruction that loads a value from a given memory address. To accomplish this, you must first load the address into a register, and then perform a register-indirect load:

```
LDR r1, =x
LDR r2, [r1]
```

A number of more complex addressing modes are available which facilitate the implementation of pointers, arrays, and structures in high level programs. Preindexing modes add a constant (or register) to a base register, and then load from the computed address:

```
LDR r1, [r2, #4] ; Load from address r2 + 4
LDR r1, [r2, r3] ; Load from address r2 + r3
```

It is also possible to write-back to the base register by appending a bang (!) character. This indicates that the computed address should be saved in the base register after the address is loaded:

```
LDR r1, [r2, #4]! ; Load from r2 + 4 then r2 += 4
LDR r1, [r2, r3]! ; Load from r2 + r3 then r2 += r3
```

Post-indexing modes do the same thing, but in the reverse order. First, the load is performed from the base register, then the base register is incremented:

```
LDR r1, [r2], #4 ; Load from r2 then r2 += 4
LDR r1, [r2], r3 ; Load from r2 then r2 += r3
```

These complex pre-indexing and post-indexing modes make it possible to have single-instruction implementations of idiomatic C operations like b = a++. The corresponding modes are also available to the STR instruction.

Absolute addresses (and other large literals) are somewhat more complicated in ARM. Because every instruction must fit into a 32-bit word, it is not possible to fit a 32-bit address into an instruction, alongside the opcode. Instead, large literals must be stored in a **literal pool**, which is a small region of data inside the code section of the program. A literal can be loaded from a pool with a PC-relative load instruction, which can reference ±4096 bytes from the loading instruction. This results in several small literal pools being scattered throughout the program, so that each one is close to the load instruction that uses it.

The ARM assembler generally hides this complexity from the user. When a label or large literal is prefixed with an equals sign, this indicates to the assembler that the marked value should be placed into a literal pool, and a corresponding PC-relative instruction emitted instead.

For example, the following instructions, which load the address of x into r1, then the value of x into r2:

```
LDR r1, =x
LDR r2, [r1]
```

Will be expanded into this load of the address of x from an adjacent literal pool, followed by loading the value of x:

```
LDR r1, .L1
LDR r2, [r1]
B   .end
.L1:
    .word x
.end:
```

10.4.3 Basic Arithmetic

ARM provides three-address arithmetic instructions on registers. The ADD and SUB instructions specify the result register as the first argument, and compute on the second and third arguments. The third operand may be an 8-bit constant, or a register with an optional shift applied. The variants with carry enabled will set or clear the C bit of the CPSR on overflow, as appropriate.

Instruction	Example
Add without carry	ADD Rd, Rm, Rn
Add with carry	ADC Rd, Rm, Rn
Subtract without carry	SUB Rd, Rm, Rn
Subtract with carry	SBC Rd, Rm, Rn

Multiplication works much the same way, except that multiplying two 32-bit numbers could result in a 64-bit value. The ordinary MUL discards the high bits of the results, while UMULL puts the 64-bit result in two 32-bit registers. The signed variant SMULL will sign extend the high register as needed.

Instruction	Example
Multiplication	MUL Rd, Rm, Rn
Unsigned Long Multiplication	UMULL RdHi, RdLo, Rm, Rn
Signed Long Multiplication	SMULL RdHi, RdLo, Rm, Rn

There is no division instruction in ARM, because it cannot be carried out in a single pipelined cycle. Instead, when division is needed, it is accomplisehd by invoking an external function in a standard library. This is left as an exercise for the reader.

The logical instructions are very similar in structure to the arithmetic instructions. We have the bitwise-and, bitwise-or, bitwise-exclusive-or and bitwise-bit-clear, which is the equivalent of a bitwise-and of the first value and the inverted second value. The move-not MVN instruction performs a bitwise-not while moving from one register to another.

Instruction	Example
Bitwise-And	AND Rd, Rm, Rn
Bitwise-Or	ORR Rd, Rm, Rn
Bitwise-Xor	EOR Rd, Rm, Rn
Bitwise-Bit-Clear	BIC Rd, RM, Rn
Move-Not	MVN Rd, Rn

10.4.4 Comparisons and Branches

The CMP instruction compares two values and sets the N (negative) and Z (zero) flags in the CPSR, to be read by later instructions. In the case of comparing a register and an immediate value, the register must be on the right had side of the comma:

```
CMP Rd, Rn
CMP Rd, #imm
```

In addition, an "S" can be appended to the arithmetic instructions to update the CPSR in a similar way. For example, SUBS will subtract two values, store the result, and update the CPSR.

Figure 10.8: ARM Branch Instructions

Opcode	Meaning		
B	Branch Always	BL	Branch and Link
BX	Branch and Exchange	BLX	Branch-Link-Exchange
BEQ	Equal	BVS	Overflow Set
BNE	Not Equal	BVC	Overflow Clear
BGT	Greater Than	BHI	Higher (unsigned $>$)
BGE	Greater Than or Equal	BHS	Higher or Same (uns. $>=$)
BLT	Less Than	BLO	Lower (unsigned $<$)
BLE	Less Than or Equal	BLS	Lower or Same (uns. $<=$)
BMI	Negative	BPL	Positive or Zero

A variety of branch instructions consult the previously-set values of the CPSR, and then jump to a given label, if the appropriate flags are set. An unconditional branch is specified with simply B.

For example, to count from zero to five:

```
        MOV  r0, #0
loop:   ADD  r0,  r0,  1
        CMP  r0,  #5
        BLT  loop
```

And to conditionally assign a global variable y ten if x is greater than 0 and 20 if it is not

```
        LDR  r0,  =x
        LDR  r0,  [r0]
        CMP  r0,  #0
        BGT  .L1
.L0:
        MOV  r0,  #20
        B    .L2
.L1:
        MOV  r0,  #10
.L2:
        LDR  r1,  =y
        STR  r0,  [r1]
```

The branch-and-link (BL) instruction, is used to implement function calls. BL sets the link register to be the address of the next instruction, and then jumps to the given label. The link register is then used as the return address at the conclusion of the function. The BX instruction branches to the address given in a register, and is most frequently used to return from a function call by branching to the link register. BLX performs a branch-and-link to the address given by a register, and can be used to invoke function pointers, virtual methods, or any other indirect jump.

A special feature of the ARM instruction set is **conditional execution**. A 4-bit field in each instruction word indicates one of 16 possible conditions that must hold, otherwise the instruction is ignored. The various types of conditional branch shown above are simply a plain branch (B) instruction with the various conditions applied. The same two letter suffixes can be applied to almost any instruction.

For example, suppose we have the following code fragment, which increments either a or b, depending on which one is smaller:

```
if(a<b) { a++; } else { b++; }
```

Instead of implementing this as control flow using branches and labels, we can simply make each of the two additions conditional upon a previous comparison. Whichever condition holds true will be executed, and the other skipped. Assuming that a and b are held in r0 and r1 respectively:

```
CMP    r0, r1
ADDLT r0, r0, #1
ADDGE r1, r1, #1
```

10.4.5 The Stack

The stack is an auxiliary data structure used primarily to record the function call history of the program along with local variables that do not fit in registers. By convention, the stack grows *downward* from high values to low values. The sp register is known as the **stack pointer** and keeps track of the bottom-most item on the stack.

To push the r0 register onto the stack, we must subtract the size of the register from sp, and then store r0 into the location pointed to by sp:

```
SUB sp, sp, #4
STR r0, [sp]
```

Alternatively, this can be done with a single instruction making use of pre-indexing and writeback:

```
STR r0, [sp, #-4]!
```

The PUSH pseudo-instruction accomplishes the same thing, but can also move any number of registers (encoded as a bitmask) to the stack. Curly braces are used to indicate the list of registers to push:

```
PUSH {r0,r1,r2}
```

Popping a value off the stack involves the opposite:

Figure 10.9: Summary of ARM Calling Convention

- The first four arguments are placed in registers r0, r1, r2 and r3.

- Additional arguments are pushed on the stack in reverse order.

- The caller must save r0-r3 and r12, if needed.

- the caller must always save r14, the link register.

- The **callee** must save r4-r11, if needed.

- The result is placed in r0.

Figure 10.10: ARM Register Assignments

Register	Purpose	Who Saves?
r0	argument 0 / result	not saved
r1	argument 1	CALLER saves
r2	argument 2	CALLER saves
r3	argument 3	CALLER saves
r4	scratch	callee saves
...	...	...
r10	scratch	callee saves
r11	frame pointer	callee saves
r12	intraprocedure	CALLER saves
r13	stack pointer	callee saves
r14	link register	CALLER saves
r15	program counter	saved in link register

```
LDR r0, [sp]
ADD sp, sp, #4
```

Once again this can be done with a single instruction:

```
LDR r0, [sp], #4
```

And, to pop a set of registers all at once:

```
POP {r0,r1,r2}
```

Unlike X86, any data items ranging from a byte to a double-word can be pushed on to the stack, as long as data alignment is respected.

10.4.6 Calling a Function

ARM uses a register calling convention described by the ARM-Thumb Procedure Call Standard (ATPCS) [4], which is summarized in Figure 10.9.

To call a function, place the desired arguments in the registers r0-r3, save the (current) value of the link register, and then use the BL instruction to jump to the function. Upon return, restore the previous value of the link register, and examine the result in register r0.

For example, the following C function:

```
int x=0;
int y=10;
int main() {
    x = printf("value: \%d\n",y);
}
```

Would become the following in ARM:

```
.data
  x:   .word 0
  y:   .word 10
  S0: .ascii "value: \%d\012\000"
.text
  main:
    LDR r0, =S0  @ Load address of S0
    LDR r1, =y   @ Load address of y
    LDR r1, [r1] @ Load value of y

    PUSH {ip,lr} @ Save registers
    BL  printf   @ Call printf
    POP  {ip,lr} @ Restore registers

    LDR r1, =x   @ Load address of x
    STR r0, [r1] @ Store return value in x
.end
```

10.4.7 Defining a Leaf Function

Because function arguments are passed in registers, it is easy to write a **leaf function** that computes a value without calling any other functions. For example, code for the following function:

```
square: function integer ( x: integer ) =
{
    return x*x;
}
```

Could be as simple as this:

```
.global square
square:
    MUL   r0, r0, r0    @ multiply argument by itself
    BX    lr            @ return to caller
```

Unfortunately, this won't work for a function that wants to invoke other functions, because we haven't set up the stack properly. A more complex approach is needed for the general case.

10.4.8 Defining a Complex Function

A complex function must be able to invoke other functions and compute expressions of arbitrary complexity, and then return to the caller with the original state intact. Consider the following recipe for a function that accepts three arguments and uses two local variables:

```
func:
    PUSH {fp}           @ save the frame pointer
    MOV  fp, sp         @ set the new frame pointer
    PUSH {r0,r1,r2}     @ save the arguments on the stack
    SUB  sp, sp, #8     @ allocate two more local variables
    PUSH {r4-r10}       @ save callee-saved registers

    @@@ body of function goes here @@@

    POP  {r4-r10}       @ restore callee saved registers
    MOV  sp, fp         @ reset stack pointer
    POP  {fp}           @ recover previous frame pointer
    BX   lr             @ return to the caller
```

Through this method, we ensure that we are able to save all the values in the registers into the stack and ensure that no data will be lost. The stack, once this has been done, looks very similar to that of the X86 stack, just with some extra callee-saved registers stored on the stack.

Here is a complete example that puts it all together. Suppose that you have a C-minor function defined as follows:

```
compute: function integer
         ( a: integer, b: integer, c: integer )
{
    int x, y;
    x = a+b+c;
    y = x*5;
    return y;
}
```

Figure 10.11: Example ARM Stack Frame

Contents	Address	
Saved r12	[fp, #8]	
Old LR	[fp, #4]	
Old Frame Pointer	[fp]	← fp points here
Argument 2	[fp, #-4]	
Argument 1	[fp, #-8]	
Argument 0	[fp, #-12]	
Local Variable 1	[fp, #-16]	
Local Variable 0	[fp, #-20]	
Saved r10	[fp, #-24]	
Saved r9	[fp, #-28]	
Saved r8	[fp, #-32]	
Saved r7	[fp, #-36]	
Saved r6	[fp, #-40]	
Saved r5	[fp, #-44]	
Saved r4	[fp, #-48]	← sp points here

A complete translation of the function is on the next page. Note that this is one of many ways to construct a valid stack frame for a function definition. Other approaches are valid, as long as the function uses the stack frame consistently. For example, the callee could first push all of the argument and scratch registers on the stack, and then allocate space for local variables below that. (The reverse process must be used on function exit, of course.)

Another common approach is for the callee PUSH {fp,ip,lr,pc} on to the stack, before pushing arguments and local variables. While not strictly required for implementing the function, it provides additional debugging information in the form of a **stack backtrace** so that a debugger can look backwards through the call stack and easily reconstruct the current execution state of the program.

The code given is correct, but rather conservative. As it turned out, this particular function didn't need to use registers r4–r5, so it wasn't necessary to save and restore them. In a similar way, we could have kept the arguments in registers without saving them to the stack. The result could have been computed directly into r0 rather than saving it to a local variable. These optimizations are easy to make when writing code by hand, but not so easy when writing a compiler.

For your first attempt at building a compiler, your code created will (probably) not be very efficient if each statement is translated independently. The preamble to a function must save all the registers, because it does not know *a priori* which registers will be used later. Likewise, a statement that computes a value must save it back to a local variable, because

Figure 10.12: Complete ARM Example

```
.globl compute
compute:
@@@@@@@@@@@@@@@@@@@@ preamble of function sets up stack
PUSH {fp}           @ save the frame pointer
MOV  fp, sp         @ set the new frame pointer
PUSH {r0,r1,r2}     @ save the arguments on the stack
SUB  sp, sp, #8     @ allocate two more local variables
PUSH {r4-r10}       @ save callee-saved registers

@@@@@@@@@@@@@@@@@@@@@@@@@ body of function starts here
LDR  r0, [fp,#-12]      @ load argument 0 (a) into r0
LDR  r1, [fp,#-8]       @ load argument 1 (b) into r1
LDR  r2, [fp,#-4]       @ load argument 2 (c) into r2
ADD  r1, r1, r2         @ add the args together
ADD  r0, r0, r1
STR  r0, [fp,#-20]      @ store the result into local 0 (x)
LDR  r0, [fp,#-20]      @ load local 0 (x) into a register.
MOV  r1, #5            @ move 5 into a register
MUL  r2, r0, r1        @ multiply both into r2
STR  r2, [fp,#-16]     @ store the result in local 1 (y)
LDR  r0, [fp,#-16]     @ move local 1 (y) into the result

@@@@@@@@@@@@@@@@@@@@@ epilogue of function restores the stack
POP  {r4-r10}       @ restore callee saved registers
MOV  sp, fp         @ reset stack pointer
POP  {fp}           @ recover previous frame pointer
BX   lr             @ return to the caller
```

it does not know beforehand whether the local will be used as a return value. We will explore these issues later in Chapter 12 on optimization.

10.4.9 64-bit Differences

The 64-bit ARMv8-A architecture provides two execution modes: The A32 mode supports the 32-bit instruction set described above, and the A64 mode supports a new 64-bit execution model. This permits a 64-bit CPU with a supporting operating system to execute a mix of 32-bit and 64-bit programs simultaneously. Though not binary compatible with A32, the A64 model follows much of the same architectural principles, with a few key changes:

Word Size. A64 instructions are still a fixed size of 32 bits, however, registers and address computations are 64 bits.

Registers. A64 has 32 64-bit registers, named x0-x31. x0 is a dedicated zero register: when read, it always provides the value zero, when written, there is no effect. x1-x15 are general purpose registers, x16 and x17 are for interprocess communication, x29 is the frame pointer, x30 is the link register and x31 is the stack pointer. (The program counter is not directly accessible from user code.) Instead of using a data type suffix, a 32-bit value may be indicated by naming a register as w#.

Instructions. A64 instructions are largely the same as A32, using the same mnemonics, with a few differences. Conditional predicates are no longer part of every instruction. Instead, all conditional codes must perform an explicit CMP and then a conditional branch. The LDM/STM instructions and pseudo-instructions PUSH/POP are not available and must be replaced with a sequence of explicit loads and stores. (This can be made more efficient by using LDP/STP which load and store pairs of registers.

Calling Convention. To invoke a function, the first eight arguments are placed in registers x0-x7, and the remainder are pushed on to the stack. The caller must preserve registers x9-x15 and x30 while the callee must preserve x19-x29. The (scalar) return value is placed in x0, while extended return values are pointed to by x8.

10.5   Further Reading

This chapter has given you a brief orientation to the core features of the X86 and ARM architectures, enough to write simple programs in the most direct way. However, you will certainly need to look up specific details of individual instructions in order to better understand their options and limitations. Now you are ready to read the detailed reference manuals and keep them handy while you construct your compiler:

1. Intel64 and IA-32 Architectures Software Developer Manuals. Intel Corp., 2017.`http://www.intel.com/content/www/us/en/processors/ architectures-software-developer-manuals.html`

2. System V Application Binary Interface, Jan Hubicka, Andreas Jaeger, Michael Matz, and Mark Mitchell (editors), 2013. `https://software. intel.com/sites/default/files/article/402129/mpx-linux64-abi. pdf`

3. ARM Architecture Reference Manual ARMv8. ARM Limited, 2017. `https://static.docs.arm.com/ddi0487/bb/DDI0487B_b_armv8_ arm.pdf.`

4. The ARM-THUMB Procedure Call Standard. ARM Limited, 2000. `http://infocenter.arm.com/help/topic/com.arm.doc.espc0002/ ATPCS.pdf.`

Chapter 11 – Code Generation

11.1   Introduction

Congratulations, you have made it to the final stage of the compiler! After scanning and parsing the source code, constructing the AST, performing type checking, and generating an intermediate representation, we are now ready to generate some code.

To start, we are going to take a naïve approach to code generation, in which we consider each element of the program in isolation. Each expression and statement will be generated as a standalone unit, without reference to its neighbors. This is easy and straightforward, but it is conservative and will lead to a large amount of non-optimal code. But it will work, and give you a starting point for thinking about more sophisticated techniques.

The examples will focus on X86-64 assembly code, but they are not hard to adapt to ARM and other assembly languages as needed. As with previous stages, we will define a method for each element of a program. `decl_codegen` will generate code for a declaration, calling `stmt_codegen` for a statement, `expr_codegen` for an expression, and so on. These relationships are shown in Figure 11.1.

Once you have learned this basic approach to code generation, you will be ready for the *following* chapter, in which we consider more complex methods for generating more highly optimized code.

11.2   Supporting Functions

Before generating some code, we need to set up a few supporting functions to keep track of a few details. To generate expressions, you will need some **scratch registers** to hold intermediate values between operators. Write three functions with the following interface:

```
int scratch_alloc();
void scratch_free( int r );
const char * scratch_name( int r );
```

Looking back at Chapter 10, you can see that we set aside each register for a purpose: some are for function arguments, some for stack frame

Figure 11.1: Code Generation Functions

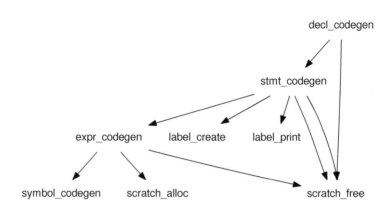

management, and some are available for scratch values. Take those scratch registers and put them into a table like this:

r	0	1	2	3	4	5	6
name	%rbx	%r10	%r11	%r12	%r13	%r14	%r15
inuse	X		X				

Then, write `scratch_alloc` to find an unused register in the table, mark it as in use, and return the register number r. `scratch_free` should mark the indicated register as available. `scratch_name` should return the name of a register, given its number r. Running out of scratch registers is possible, but unlikely, as we will see below. For now, if `scratch_alloc` cannot find a free register, just emit an error message and halt.

Next, we will need to generate a large number of unique, anonymous labels that indicate the targets of jumps and conditional branches. Write two functions to generate and display labels:

```
int label_create();
const char * label_name( int label );
```

`label_create` simply increments a global counter and returns the current value. `label_name` returns that label in a string form, so that label 15 is represented as ``.L15''.

Finally, we need a way of mapping from the symbols in a program to the assembly language code representing those symbols. For this, write a function to generate the address of a symbol:

```
const char * symbol_codegen( struct symbol *s );
```

This function returns a string which is a fragment of an instruction, representing the address computation needed for a given symbol. Write symbol_codegen to first examine the scope of the symbol. Global variables are easy: the name in assembly language is the same as in the source language. If you have a symbol structure representing the global variable count:integer, then symbol_codegen should simply return count.

Symbols that represent local variables and function parameters should instead return an address computation that yields the position of that local variable or parameter on the stack. The groundwork for this was laid in the typechecking phase, where you assigned each symbol a unique number, starting with the parameters and continuing with each local variable.

For example, suppose you have this function definition:

```
f: function void ( x: integer, y: integer )
{
    z: integer = 10;
    return x + y + z;
}
```

In this case, x was assigned a position of zero, y is position one, and z is position two. Now look back at Figure 10.5, which shows the stack layout on the X86-64 processor. Position zero is at the address -8(%rbp), position one is at -16(%rbp), and position two is at -24(%rbp).

Given that, you can now extend symbol_codegen to return a string describing the precise stack address of local variables and parameters, knowing only its position in the stack frame.

11.3 Generating Expressions

The basic approach to generating assembly code for an expression is to perform a post-order traversal of the AST or DAG, and emit one or more instructions for each node. The main idea is to keep track of the registers in which each intermediate value is stored. To do this, add a reg field to the AST or DAG node structure, which will hold the number of a register returned by scratch_alloc. As you visit each node, emit an instruction and place into the reg field the number of the register containing that value. When the node is no longer needed, call scratch_free to release it.

Suppose we want to generate X86 code for the following DAG, where a, b and c are global integers:

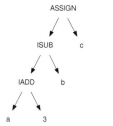

```
1.  MOVQ   a,  R0
2.  MOVQ  $3,  R1
3.  ADDQ  R0,  R1
4.  MOVQ   b,  R0
5.  SUBQ  R0,  R1
6.  MOVQ  R1,  c
```

Figure 11.2: Example of Generating X86 Code from a DAG

A post-order traversal would visit the nodes in the following order:

1. Visit the a node. Call scratch_alloc to allocate a new register (0) and save that in node->reg. Then emit the instruction MOVQ a, R0 to load the value into register zero. [1]

2. Visit the 3 node. Call scratch_alloc to allocate a new register (1) and emit the instruction MOVQ $3, R1.

3. Visit the IADD node. By examining the two children of this node, we can see that their values are stored in registers R0 and R1, so we emit an instruction that adds them together: ADDQ R0, R1. This is a destructive two-address instruction which leaves the result in R1. R0 is no longer needed, so we call scratch_free(0).

4. Visit the b node. Call scratch_alloc to allocate a new register (0) and emit MOVQ b, R0.

5. Visit the ISUB node. Emit SUBQ R0, R1, leaving the result in R1, and freeing register R0.

6. Visit the c node, but don't emit anything, because it is the target of the assignment.

7. Visit the ASSIGN node and emit MOVQ R1, c.

---

[1]Note that the actual name of register R0 is scratch_name(0), which is %ebx. To keep the example clear, we will call them R0, R1, etc for now.

And here is the same code with the actual register names provided by scratch_name:

```
MOVQ      a,  %rbx
MOVQ     $3,  %r10
ADDQ  %r10,  %rbx
MOVQ      b,  %rbx
SUBQ  %rbx,  %r10
MOVQ  %r10,  c
```

Here is how to implement it in code. Write a function called expr_codegen that first recursively calls expr_codegen for its left and right children. This will cause each child to generate code such that the result will be left in the register number noted in the register field. The current node then generates code using those registers, and frees the registers it no longer needs. Figure 11.3 gives a skeleton for this approach.

A few additional refinements are needed to the basic process.

First, not all symbols are simple global variables. When a symbol forms part of an instruction, use symbol_codegen to return the string that gives the specific address for that symbol. For example, if a was the first parameter to the function, then the first instruction in the sequence would have looked like this instead:

```
MOVQ  -8(%rbp),  %rbx
```

Second, some nodes in the DAG may require multiple instructions, so as to handle peculiarities of the instruction set. You will recall that the X86 IMUL only takes one argument, because the first argument is always %rax and the result is always placed in %rax with the overflow in %rdx. To perform the multiply, we must move one child register into %rax, multiply by the other child register, and then move the result from %rax to the destination scratch register. For example, the expression (x*10) would translate as this:

```
MOV  $10,  %rbx
MOV    x,  %r10
MOV  %rbx,  %rax
IMUL  %r10
MOV  %rax,  %r11
```

Of course, this also means that %rax and %rdx cannot be used for other purposes while a multiply is in progress. Since we have a large number of scratch registers to work with, we will just not use %rdx for any other purpose in our basic code generator.

```
void expr_codegen( struct expr *e )
{
    if(!e) return;

    switch(e->kind) {

        // Leaf node: allocate register and load value.

        case EXPR_NAME:
            e->reg = scratch_alloc();
            printf("MOVQ %s, %s\n",
                symbol_codegen(e->symbol),
                scratch_name(e->reg));
            break;

        // Interior node: generate children, then add them.

        case EXPR_ADD:
            expr_codegen(e->left);
            expr_codegen(e->right);
            printf("ADDQ %s, %s\n",
                scratch_name(e->left->reg),
                scratch_name(e->right->reg));
            e->reg = e->right->reg;
            scratch_free(e->left->reg);
            break;

        case EXPR_ASSIGN:
            expr_codegen(e->left);
            printf("MOVQ %s, %s\n",
                scratch_name(e->left->reg),
                symbol_codegen(e->right->symbol));
            e->reg = e->left->reg;
            break;
        . . .
    }
}
```

Figure 11.3: Expression Generation Skeleton

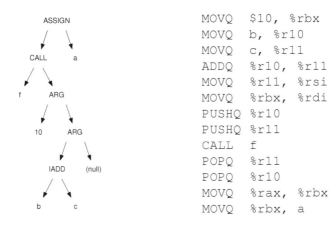

```
MOVQ  $10, %rbx
MOVQ  b, %r10
MOVQ  c, %r11
ADDQ  %r10, %r11
MOVQ  %r11, %rsi
MOVQ  %rbx, %rdi
PUSHQ %r10
PUSHQ %r11
CALL  f
POPQ  %r11
POPQ  %r10
MOVQ  %rax, %rbx
MOVQ  %rbx, a
```

Figure 11.4: Generating Code for a Function Call

Third, how do we invoke a function? Recall that a function is repre-sented by a single CALL node, with each of the arguments in an unbal-anced tree of ARG nodes. Figure 11.4 gives an example of a DAG repre-senting the expression `a=f(10,b+c)`

The code generator must evaluate each of the ARG nodes, computing the value of each left hand child. If the machine has a stack calling con-vention, then each ARG node corresponds to a PUSH onto the stack. If the machine has a register calling convention, generate all of the arguments, then copy each one into the appropriate argument register after all argu-ments are generated. Then, emit CALL on the function name, after saving any caller-saved registers. When the function call returns, move the value from the return register (`%rax`) into a newly allocated scratch register and restore the caller-saved registers.

Finally, note carefully the side effects of expression. Every expression has a **value** which is computed and left in a scratch register for its parent node to consider. Some expressions also have **side effects** which are ac-tions in addition to the value. With some operators, it is easy to overlook one or the other!

For example, the expression `(x=10)` yields a *value* of 10, which means you can use that expression anywhere a value is expected. This is what allows you to write `y=x=10` or `f(x=10)`. The expression also has the *side effect* of storing the value 10 into the variable x. When you generate code for `x=10` assignment, be sure to carry out the side effect of storing 10 into x (that's obvious) but also retain the value 10 in the register that represents the value of the expression.

11.4   Generating Statements

Now that we have encapsulated expression generation into a single function `expr_codegen`, we can begin to build up larger code structures that rely upon expressions. `stmt_codegen` will create code for all control flow statements. Begin by writing a skeleton for `stmt_codegen` like this:

```
void stmt_codegen( struct stmt *s )
{
    if(!s) return;

    switch(s->kind) {
        case STMT_EXPR:
            ...
            break;
        case STMT_DECL:
            ...
            break;
        ...
    }
    stmt_codegen(s->next);
}
```

Figure 11.5: Statement Generator Skeleton

Now consider each kind of statement in turn, starting with the easy cases. If the statement describes a declaration STMT_DECL of a local variable, then just delegate that by calling `decl_codegen`:

```
case STMT_DECL:
    decl_codegen(s->decl);
    break;
```

A statement that consists of an expression (STMT_EXPR) simply requires that we call `expr_codegen` on that expression, and then free the scratch register containing the top-level value of the expression. (In fact, every time `expr_codegen` is called, a scratch register should be freed.)

```
case STMT_EXPR:
    expr_codegen(s->expr);
    scratch_free(s->expr->reg);
    break;
```

A `return` statement must evaluate an expression, move it into the designated register for return values `%rax`, and then jump to the function epilogue, which will unwind the stack and return to the call point. (See below for more details about the prologue.)

```
case STMT_RETURN:
    expr_codegen(s->expr);
    printf("MOV %s, %%rax\n",scratch_name(s->expr->reg));
    printf("JMP .%s_epilogue\n",function_name);
    scratch_free(s->expr->reg);
    break;
```

(The careful reader will notice that this code needs to know the name of the function that contains this statement. You will have to figure out a way to pass that information down.)

Control flow statements are more interesting. It's useful to first consider what we want the output assembly language to look like, and then work backwards to get the code for generating it.

Here is a template for a conditional statement:

if (*expr* **) {**
     true-statements
} else {
     false-statements
}

To express this in assembly, we must evaluate the control expression so that its value resides in a known register. A CMP expression is then used to test if the value is equal to zero (false). If the expression is false, then we must jump to the false branch of the statement with a JE (jump-if-equal) statement. Otherwise, we continue through to the true branch of the statement. At the end of the true statement, we must JMP over the else body to the end of the statement.

     expr
     CMP *register*, $0
     JE *false-label*
     true-statements
     JMP *done-label*
false-label :
     false-statements
done-label :

Once you have a skeleton of the desired code, writing the code generator is easy. First, generate two new labels, then call `expr_codegen` for each expression, `stmt_codegen` for each statement, and substitute the few additional instructions as needed to make the overall structure.

```
case STMT_IF:
    int else_label = label_create();
    int done_label = label_create();
    expr_codegen(s->expr);
    printf("CMP %s, $0\n",scratch_name(s->expr->reg));
    scratch_free(s->expr->reg);
    printf("JE   %s\n",label_name(else_label));
    stmt_codegen(s->body);
    printf("JMP %s\n",label_name(done_label));
    printf("%s:\n",label_name(else_label));
    stmt_codegen(s->else_body);
    printf("%s:\n",label_name(done_label));
    break;
```

A similar approach can be used to generate loops. Here is the source template of a for-loop:

for (init-expr **;** expr **;** next-expr **) {**
     body-statements
}

And here is the corresponding assembly template. First, evaluate the initializing expression. Then, upon each iteration of the loop, evaluate the control expression. If false, jump to the end of the loop. If not, execute the body of the loop, then evaluate the next expression.

     init-expr
top-label:
     expr
     CMP register, $0
     JE   done-label
     body-statements
     next-expression
     JMP top-label
done-label :

Writing the code generator is left as an exercise for the reader. Just keep in mind that each of the three expressions in a for-loop can be omitted. If the *init-expr* or the *next-expr* are omitted, they have no effect. if the *expr* is omitted, it is assumed to be true. [2]

Many languages have loop-control constructs like `continue;` and `break;`. In these cases, the compiler must keep track of the labels associated with the current loop being generated, and convert these into a JMP to the top label, or the done-label respectively.

The `print` statement in B-Minor is a special case of an imperative statement with variant behavior depending on the type of the expression to be printed. For example, the following `print` statement must generate slightly different code for the integer, boolean, and string to be printed:

```
i: integer = 10;
b: boolean = true;
s: string = "\n";
print i, b, s;
```

Obviously, there is no simple assembly code corresponding to the display of an integer. In this case, a common approach is to reduce the task into an abstraction that we already know. The printing of integers, booleans, strings, etc, can be delegated to function calls that explicitly perform those actions. The generated code for `print i, b, s` is then equivalent to this:

```
print_integer(i);
print_boolean(b);
print_string(s);
```

So, to generate a `print` statement, we simply generate the code for each expression to be printed, determine the type of the expression with `expr_typecheck` and then emit the corresponding function call.

Of course, each of these functions must be written and then linked into each instance of a B-Minor program, so they are available when needed. These functions, and any others necessary, are collectively known as the **runtime library** for B-Minor programs. As a general rule, the more high-level a programming language, the more runtime support is needed.

---

[2]Yes, each of the three components of a for-loop are expressions. It is customary that the first has a side effect of initialization ($i=0$)), the second is a comparison ($i<10$), and the third has a side effect to generate the next value ($i++$), but they are all just plain expressions.

11.5 Conditional Expressions

Now that you know how to generate control flow statements, we must return to one aspect of expression generation. Conditional expressions (less-than, greater-than, equals, etc) compare two values and return a boolean value. They most frequently appear in control flow expressions but can also be used as simple values, like this:

```
b: boolean = x < y;
```

The problem is that there is no single instruction that simply performs the comparison and places the boolean result in a register. Instead, you must go the long way around and make a control flow construct that compares the two expressions, then constructs the desired result.

For example, if you have a conditional expression like this:

| left-expr | < | right-expr |

then generate code according to this template:

| left-expr |
| right-expr |

CMP *left-register right-register*
JLT *true-label*
MOV *false, result-register*
JMP *done-label*
true-label:
    MOV *true, result-register*
done-label:

Of course, for different conditional operators, use a different jump instruction in the appropriate place. With slight variations, you can use the same approach to implement the ternary conditional operator (x?a:b) found in many languages.

A funny outcome of this approach is that if you generate code for an if-statement like if (x>y) {...} in the obvious way, you will end up with *two* conditional structures in the assembly code. The first conditional computes the result of x>y and places that in a register. The second conditional compares that results against zero and then jumps to the true or false branch of the statement. With a little careful coding, you can check for this common case and generate a single conditional statement that evaluates the expression and uses one conditional jump to implement the statement.

11.6 Generating Declarations

Finally, emitting the entire program is a matter of traversing each declaration of code or data and emitting its basic structure. Declarations can fall into three cases: global variable declarations, local variable declarations, and global function declarations. (B-Minor does not permit local function declarations.)

Global data declarations are simply a matter of emitting a label along with a suitable directive that reserves the necessary space, and an initializer, if needed. For example, these B-Minor declarations at global scope:

```
i: integer = 10;
s: string = "hello";
b: array [4] boolean = {true, false, true, false};
```

Should yield these output directives:

```
.data
i:   .quad 10
s:   .string "hello"
b:   .quad 1, 0, 1, 0
```

Note that a global variable declaration can only be initialized by a constant value (and not a general expression) precisely because the data section of the program can only contain constants (and not code). If the programmer accidentally put code into the initializer, then the typechecker should have discovered that and raised an error before code generation began.

Emitting a local variable declaration is much easier. (This only happens when decl_codegen is called by stmt_codegen inside of a function declaration.) Here, you can assume that space for the local variable has already been established by the function prologue, so no stack manipulations are necessary. However, if the variable declaration has an initializing expression (x:integer=y*10;) then you must generate code for the expression, store it in the local variable, and free the register.

Function declarations are the final piece. To generate a function, you must emit a label with the function's name, followed by the function prologue. The prologue must take into account the number of parameters and local variables, making the appropriate amount of space on the stack. Next comes the body of the function, followed by the function epilogue. The epilogue should have a unique label so that return statements can easily jump there.

11.7 Exercises

1. Write a legal expression that would exhaust the six available scratch registers, if using the technique described in this chapter. In general, how many registers are needed to generate code for an arbitrary expression tree?

2. When using a register calling convention, why is it necessary to generate values for *all* the function arguments before moving the values into the argument registers?

3. Can a global variable declaration have a non-constant initializing expression? Explain why.

4. Suppose B-Minor included a `switch` statement. Sketch out two different assembly language templates for implementing a `switch`.

5. Write the complete code generator for the X86-64 architecture, as outlined in this chapter.

6. Write several test programs to test all the aspects of B-Minor then use your compiler to build, test, and run them.

7. Compare the assembly output of your compiler on your test programs to the output of a production compiler like `gcc` on equivalent programs written in C. What differences do you see?

8. Add an extra code generator to your compiler that emits a different assembly language like ARM or an intermediate representation like LLVM. Describe any changes in approach that were necessary.

Chapter 12 – Optimization

12.1 Overview

Using the basic code generation strategy shown in the previous chapter, you can build a compiler that will produce perfectly usable, working code. However, if you examine the output of your compiler, there are many ways in which you can see obvious inefficiencies. This stems from the fact that the basic code generation strategy considers each program element in isolation, and must use the most conservative strategy to connect them together.

In the early days of high level languages, before optimization strategies were widespread, code produced by compilers was widely seen to be inferior to that which was hand-written by humans. Today, a modern compiler has many optimization techniques and very detailed knowledge of the underlying architecture, and so compiled code is usually (but not always) superior to that written by humans.

Optimizations can be applied at multiple stages of the compiler. It's usually best to solve a problem at the highest level of abstraction possible. For example, once we have generated concrete assembly code, about the most we can do is eliminate a few redundant instructions. But, if we work with a linear IR, we can speed up a long code sequence with smart register allocation. And if we work at the level of a DAG or an AST, we can eliminate entire chunks of unused code.

Optimizations can occur at different scope within a program. **Local optimizations** refer to changes that are limited to a single basic block, which is a straight-line sequence of code without any flow control. **Global optimizations** refer to changes applied to the entire body of a function (or procedure, method, etc), consisting of a control-flow-graph where each node is a basic block. **Interprocedural optimizations** are even larger, and take into account the relationships between different functions. Generally, optimizations at larger scopes are more challenging, but have more potential to improve the program.

This chapter will give you a tour of some common code optimization techniques that you can either implement in your project compiler, or explore by implementing them by hand. But this is just an introduction: code optimization is a very large topic that could occupy a whole second textbook, and is still an area of active research today. If this chapter appeals to you, then check out some of the more advanced books and articles referenced at the end of the chapter.

12.2   Optimization in Perspective

As a programmer – the user of a compiler – it's important to keep a sense of perspective about compiler optimizations. Most production compilers do not perform any major optimizations when run with the default options. There are several reasons for this. One reason is compilation time: when initially developing and debugging a program, you want to be able to edit, compile, and test many times rapidly. Almost all optimizations require additional compilation time, which doesn't help in the initial development phases of a program. Another reason is that not all optimizations automatically improve a program: they may cause it to use more memory, or even run longer! Yet a third reason is that optimizations can confuse debugging tools, making it difficult to relate program execution back to the source code.

Thus, if you have a program that doesn't run as fast as you would like, it's best to stop and think about your program from first principles. Two suggestions to keep in mind:

- Examine the overall algorithmic complexity of your program: a binary search ($O(\log n)$) is always going to outperform a linear search ($O(n)$) for sufficiently large n. Improving the high level approach of your program is likely to yield much greater benefits than a low-level optimization.

- Measure the performance of your program. Use a standard profiling tool like `gprof` [4] to measure where, exactly, your program spends most of its time, and then focus your efforts on improving that one piece of code by either rewriting it, or enabling the appropriate compiler optimizations.

Once your program is well-written from first principles, then it is time to think about enabling specific compiler optimizations. Most optimizations are designed to target a certain pattern of behavior of code, and so you may find it helpful to write your code in those easily-identified patterns. In fact, most of the patterns discussed below can be performed by hand without the compiler's help, allowing you to do a head-to-head comparison of different code patterns.

Of course, the fragments of code presented in this chapter are all quite small, and thus are only significant if they are performed a large number of times within a program. This typically happens inside one or more nested loops that constitute the main activity of a program, often called the **kernel** of a computation. To measure the cost of, say, multiplying two

```
#include <time.h>

struct timeval start,stop,elapsed;
gettimeofday(&start,0);

for(i=0;i<1000000;i++) {
    x = x * y;
}

gettimeofday(&stop,0);
timersub(&stop,&start,&elapsed);

printf("elapsed: %d.%06d sec",
        elapsed.tv_sec,elapsed.tv_usec);
```

Figure 12.1: Timing a Fast Operation

values together, perform it one million times within a timer interval, as shown in Figure 12.1

Careful: The timer will count not only the action in the loop, but also the code implementing the loop, so you also need to normalize the result by subtracting the runtime of an empty loop.

12.3   High Level Optimizations

12.3.1   Constant Folding

Good programming practices often encourage the liberal use of named constants throughout to clarify the purpose and meaning of values. For example, instead of writing out the obscure number 86400, one might write out the following expression to yield the same number:

```
const int seconds_per_minute=60;
const int minutes_per_hour=60;
const int hours_per_day=24;

int seconds_per_day = seconds_per_minute
                    * minutes_per_hour
                    * hours_per_day;
```

The end result is the same (86400) but the code is much clearer about the purpose and origin of that number. However, if translated literally, the program would contain three excess constants, several memory lookups, and two multiplications to obtain the same result. If done in the inner loop of a complex program, this could be a significant waste. Ideally, it

```
struct expr * expr_fold( struct expr *e )
{
    expr_fold( e->left )
    expr_fold( e->right )

    if( e->left and e->right are both constants ) {

        f = expr_create( EXPR_CONSTANT );
        f->value = e->operator applied to
                    e->left->value and e->right->value
        expr_delete(e->left);
        expr_delete(e->right);

        return f;
    } else {
        return e;
    }
}
```

Figure 12.2: Constant Folding Pseudo-Code

should be possible for the programmer to be verbose without resulting in an inefficient program.

Constant folding is the technique of converting an expression (or part of an expression) combining multiple constants into a single constant. An operator node in the tree with two constant child nodes can be converted into a single node with the result of the operation computed in advance. The process can cascade up so that complex expressions may be reduced to a single constant. In effect, it moves some of the program's work from execution-time to compile-time.

This can be implemented by a recursive function that performs a post order traversal of the expression tree. Figure 12.2 gives pseudo code for constant folding on the AST.

One must be careful that the resulted computed in advance is *precisely* equal to what would have been performed at runtime. This requires using variables of the same precision and dealing with boundary cases such as underflow, overflow, and division by zero. In those cases, it is typical to force a compile-time error, rather than compute an unexpected result.

While the effects of constant folding may seem minimal, it often is the first step in enabling a chain of further optimizations.

12.3.2 Strength Reduction

Strength reduction is the technique of converting a special case of an expensive operation into a less expensive operation. For example, the source code expression x^y for exponentiation on floating point values is, in general, implemented as a call to the function pow(x,y), which might be implemented as an expansion of a Taylor series. However, in the particular case of x^2 we can substitute the expression x*x which accomplishes the same thing, avoiding the extra cost of a function call and many loop iterations. In a similar way, multiplication/division by any power of two can be replaced with a bitwise left/right shift, respectively. For example, x*8 can be replaced with x<<3.

Some compilers also contain rules for strength reduction of operations in the standard library. For example, recent versions of gcc will substitute a call to printf(s) with a constant string s to the equivalent call to puts(s). In this case, the strength reduction comes from reducing the amount of code that must be linked into the program: puts is very simple, while printf has a large number of features and further code dependencies.[1]

12.3.3 Loop Unrolling

Consider the common construct of using a loop to compute variations of a simple expression many times:

```
for(i=0;i<400;i++) {
    a[i] = i*2 + 10;
}
```

In any assembly language, this will only require a few instructions in the loop body to compute the value of a[i] each time. But, the instructions needed to control the loop will be a significant fraction of the execution time: each time through the loop, we must check whether i<400 and jump back to the top of the loop.

Loop unrolling is the technique of transforming a loop into another that has fewer iterations, but does more work per iteration. The number repetitions within the loop is known as the **unrolling factor**. The example above could be safely transformed to this:

```
for(i=0;i<400;i+=4) {
    a[i]   = i*2 + 10;
    a[i+1] = (i+1)*2 + 10;
    a[i+2] = (i+2)*2 + 10;
```

---

[1]While there is a logic to this sort of optimization, it does seem like an unseemly level of familiarity between the compiler and the standard library, which may have different developers and evolve independently.

```
    a[i+3] = (i+3)*2 + 10;
}
```

Or this:

```
for(i=0;i<400;i++) {
    a[i] = i*2 + 10;
    i++;
    a[i] = i*2 + 10;
    i++;
    a[i] = i*2 + 10;
    i++;
    a[i] = i*2 + 10;
}
```

Increasing the work per loop iteration saves some unnecessary evaluations of i<400, and it also eliminates branches from the instruction stream, which avoids pipeline stalls and other complexities within the microprocessor.

But how much should a loop be unrolled? The unrolled loop could contain 4, 8, 16 or even more items per iteration. In the extreme case, the compiler could eliminate the loop entirely and replace it with a finite sequence of statements, each with a constant value:

```
a[0] = 0 + 10;
a[1] = 2 + 10;
a[2] = 4 + 10;
. . .
```

As the unrolling factor increases, unnecessary work in the loop structures are eliminated. However, the increasing code size has its own cost: instead of reading the same instructions over and over again, the processor must keep loading new instructions from memory. If the unrolled loop results in a working set larger than the instruction cache, then performance may end *worse* than the original code.

For this reason, there are no hard-and-fast rules on when to use loop unrolling. Compilers often have global options for unrolling that can be modified by a #pragma placed before a specific loop. Manual experimentation may be needed to get good results for a specific program. [2]

12.3.4 Code Hoisting

Sometimes, code fragments inside a loop are constant with each iteration of the loop. In this case, it is unnecessary to recompute on every iteration,

---

[2]The GCC manual has this to say about the -funroll-all-loops option: "This usually makes programs run more slowly."

and so the code can be moved to the block preceding the loop, which is known as **code hoisting**. For example, the array index in this example is constant throughout the loop, and can be computed once before the loop body:

```
for(i=0;i<400;i++) {          t = x*y;
    a[x*y] += i;              for(i=0;i<400;i++) {
}                                 a[t] += i;
                              }
```

Unlike loop unrolling, code hoisting is a relatively benign optimization. The only cost to the optimization is that the computed result must occupy either a temporary location for the duration of the loop, which slightly increases either register pressure or local storage consumption. This is offset by the elimination of unnecessary computation.

12.3.5 Function Inlining

Function inlining is the process of substituting a function call with the effect of that function call directly in the code. This is particularly useful for brief functions that exist to improve the clarity or modularity of code, but do not perform a large amount of computation. For example, suppose that the simple function quadratic is called from many times within a loop, like this:

```
int quadratic( int a, int b, int x ) {
    return a*x*x + b*x + 30;
}

for(i=0;i<1000;i++) {
    y = quadratic(10,20,i*2);
}
```

The overhead of setting up the parameters and invoking the function likely exceeds the cost of doing the handful of additions and multiplies within the function itself. By inlining the function code into the loop, we can improve the overall performance of the program.

Function inlining is most easily performed on a high level representation such as an AST or a DAG. First, the body of the function must be duplicated, then the parameters of the invocation must be substituted in. Note that, at this level of evaluation, the parameters are not necessarily constants, but may be complex expressions that contain unbound values.

For example, the invocation of quadratic above can be substituted with the expression (a*x*x+b*x+30) under the binding of a=10, b=20, and x=i*2. Once this substitution is performed, unbound variables such as i are relative to the scope where quadratic was called, not where it was defined. The resulting code looks like this:

```
for(i=0;i<1000;i++) {
    y = 10*(i*2)*(i*2) + 20*(i*2) + 30;
}
```

This example highlights a hidden potential cost of function inlining: an expression (like i*2) which was previously evaluated once and then used as a parameter to the function, is now evaluated multiple times, which could increase the cost of the expression. On the other hand, this expansion could be offset by algebraic optimizations which now have the opportunity to simplify the combination of the function with its concrete parameters. For example, constant folding applied to the above example yields this:

```
for(i=0;i<1000;i++) {
    y = 40*i*i + 40*i + 30;
}
```

Generally speaking, function inlining is best applied to simple leaf functions that are called frequently and do little work relative to the cost of invocation. However, making this determination automatically is challenging to get right, because the benefits are relatively clear, but the costs in terms of increased code size and duplicated evaluations are not so easy to quantify. As a result, many languages offer a keyword (like inline in C and C++) that allow the programmer to make this determination manually.

12.3.6 Dead Code Detection and Elimination

It is not uncommon for a compiled program to contain some amount of code that is completely unreachable and will not be executed under any possible input. This could be as simple as a mistake by the programmer, who by accident returned from a function before the final statement. Or, it could be due to the application of multiple optimizations in sequence that eventually result in a branch that will never be executed. Either way, the compiler can help by flagging it for the programmer or removing it outright.

Dead code detection is typically performed on a **control flow graph** after constant folding and other expression optimizations have been performed. For example, consider the following code fragment and its control flow graph:

```
if ( x<y ) {
    return 10;
} else {
    print "hello";
}
print "goodbye";
return 30;
```

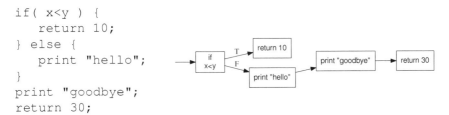

A `return` statement causes an immediate termination of the function and (from the perspective of the control flow graph) is the end of the execution path. Here, the true branch of the `if` statement immediately returns, while the false branch falls through to the next statement. For *some* values of x and y, it is possible to reach every statement.

However, if we make a slight change, like this:

```
if ( x<y ) {
    return 10;
} else {
    return 20;
}
print "goodbye";
return 30;
```

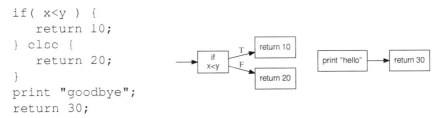

Then, both branches of the if statement terminate in a `return`, and it is not possible to reach the final `print` and `return` statements. This is (likely) a mistake by the programmer and should be flagged.

Once the control flow graph is created, determining reachability is simple: perform a traversal of the CFG, starting from the entry point of the function, marking each node as it is visited. Once the traversal is complete, if there are any nodes unmarked, then they are unreachable and the compiler may either generate a suitable error message or simply not generate code for the unreachable portion. [3]

Reachability analysis becomes particularly powerful when combined with other forms of static analysis. In the example above, suppose that variables x and y are defined as constants `100` and `200`, respectively. Constant folding can reduce x<y to simply `true`, with the result that the false branch of the if statement is never taken and therefore unreachable.

Now, don't get carried away with this line of thinking. If you were paying attention in your theory-of-computing course, this may sound suspiciously like the Halting Problem: can we determine whether an *arbitrary* program written in a Turing-complete language will run to completion, without actually executing it? The answer is, of course, *no, not in the general case.* Reachability analysis simply determines *in some limited cases*

---

[3]A slight variation on this technique can be used to evaluate whether every code path through a function results in a suitable `return` statement. This is left as an exercise to the reader.

that a certain branch of a program is impossible to take, regardless of the prorgam input. It does *not* state that the "reachable" branches of the program *will* be taken for some input, or for any input at all.

12.4   Low-Level Optimizations

All of the optimizations discussed so far can be applied to the high level structure of a program, without taking into account the particular target machine. Low-level optimizations focus more on the translation of the program structure in a way that best exploits the peculiarities of the underlying machine.

12.4.1   Peephole Optimizations

Peephole optimizations refer to any optimization that looks very narrowly at a small section of code – perhaps just two or three instructions – and makes a safe, focused change within that section. These sort of optimizations are very easy to implement as the final stage of compilation, but have a limited overall effect.

Redundant load elimination is a common peephole optimization. A sequence of expressions that both modifies and uses the same variable can easily result in two adjacent instructions that save a register into memory, and then immediately load the same value again:

Before: **After:**

```
MOVQ %R8, x                        MOVQ %R8, x
MOVQ x, %R8
```

A slight variation is that a load to a different register can be converted into a direct move between registers, thus saving an unnecessary load and pipeline stall:

Before: **After:**

```
MOVQ %R8, x                        MOVQ %R8, x
MOVQ x, %R9                        MOVQ %R8, %R9
```

12.4.2   Instruction Selection

In Chapter 11, we presented a simple method of code generation where each node of the AST (or DAG) was replaced with at least one instruction (and in some cases, multiple instructions). In a rich CISC instruction set, a single instruction can easily combine multiple operations, such as dereferencing a pointer, accessing memory, and performing an arithmetic operation.

To exploit these powerful instructions, we can use the technique of instruction selection by **tree coverage**. [5] The idea is to first represent each possible instruction in the architecture as a template tree, where the leaves can be registers, constants, or memory addresses that can be substituted into an instruction.

For example, one variant of the X86 ADDQ instruction can add two registers together. This can be used to implement an IADD node in the DAG, provided the leaves of the IADD are stored in registers. Once the add is complete, the ADDQ places the result in the same register as the second argument. This is all expressed as tree fragment that matches a part of the DAG, and an instruction to be emitted, once specific register numbers are chosen:

ADDQ C_j, R_i

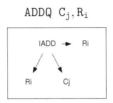

Figure 12.3 gives a few more examples of X86 instructions that can be represented as tree templates. The simple instructions at the top simply substitute one entity in the DAG for another: MOV $Cj, Ri converts a constant into a register, while MOV Mx, Ri converts a memory location into a register. Richer instructions have more structure: the complex load MOV Cd(Rc,Ra,8), Ri can be used to represent a combination of add, multiply, and dereference.

Of course, Figure 12.3 is not the complete X86 instruction set. To describe even a significant subset would require hundreds of entries, with multiple entries per instruction to capture the multiple variations on each instruction. (For example, you would need one template for an ADDQ on two registers, and another for a register-memory combination.) But this is a feasible task and perhaps easier to accomplish than hand-writing a complete code generator.

With the complete library of templates written, the job of the code generator is to examine the tree for sub-trees that match an instruction template. When one is found, the corresponding instruction is emitted (with appropriate substitutions for register numbers, etc) and the matching portion of the tree replaced with the right side of the template.

For example, suppose we wish to generate X86 code for the statement a[i] = b + 1; Let us suppose that b is a global variable, while a and i are local variables at positions 40 and 32 above the base pointer, respectively. Figure 12.4 shows the steps of tree rewriting. In each DAG, the box indicates the subtree that matches a rule in Figure 12.3

Step 1: The left IADD should be executed first to compute the value of the expression. Looking at our table of templates, there is no IADD that can directly add a memory location to a constant. So, we instead select rule (2), which emits the instruction MOVQ b, %R0 and converts the left-hand

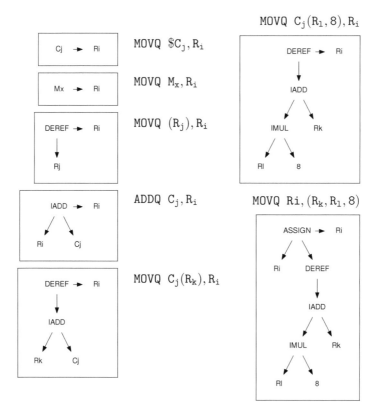

Figure 12.3: Example X86 Instruction Templates

side of the template (a memory location) into the right hand side (register %R0).

Step 2: Now we can see an IADD of a register and a constant, which matches the template of rule (4). We emit the instruction ADDQ $1, %R0 and replace the IADD subtree with the register %R0.

Step 3: Now let's look at the other side of the tree. We can use rule (5) to match the entire subtree that loads the variable i from %RBP+32 by emitting the instruction MOVQ 32(%RBP), %R1 and replacing the subtree with the register %R1.

Step 4: In a similar way, we can use rule (6) to compute the address of a by emitting LEAQ 40(%RBP), %R2. Notice that this is, in effect, a three-address addition specialized for use with a register and a constant.

Step 5: Finally, template rule (7) matches most of what is remaining. We can emit MOVQ R0, (R1,8)%R2 which stores the value in R1 into the computed array address of a. The left side of the template is replaced with the right-hand side, leaving nothing but the register %R0. With the tree

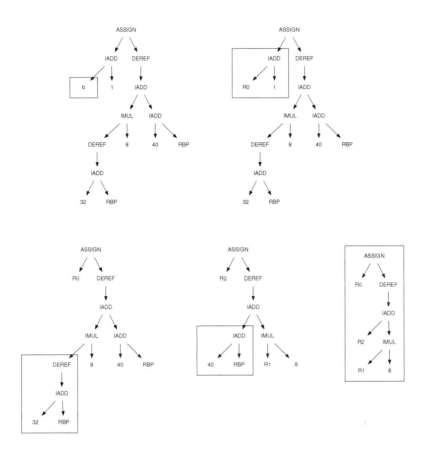

Figure 12.4: Example of Tree Rewriting

completely reduced to a single register, code generation is complete, and register %R0 can be freed.

Under the simple code generation scheme, this 16-node DAG would have produced (at least) 16 instructions of output. By using tree coverage, we reduced the output to these five instructions:

```
MOVQ  b,%R0
ADDQ  $1,%R0
MOVQ  32(%RBP),%R1
LEAQ  40(%RBP),%R2
MOVQ  %R0,(%R2,%R1,8)
```

12.5   Register Allocation

In modern CPUs, on-chip computational speed far outstrips memory latency: thousands of arithmetic operations can be completed in the time it takes to perform a single load of store. It follows that any optimizations that eliminates a load or store from memory can have a considerable impact on the performance of a program. Eliminating completely unnecessary code and variables is the first step towards doing this.

The next step is to assign specific local variables into registers, so they never need to be loaded from or stored to memory. Of course, there are a limited number of registers and not every variable can claim one. The process of **register allocation** is to identify the variables that are the best candidates for locating in registers instead of memory.

The mechanics of converting a variable into a register are straightforward. In each case where a value would be loaded from or stored into a memory location, the compiler simply substitutes the assigned register as the location of the value, so that it is used directly as the source or target of an instruction. The more complicated questions relate to whether it is *safe* to registerize a variable, which variables are most *important* to registerize, and which variables can coexist in registers at once. Let's look at each qeustion in turn.

12.5.1   *Safety of Register Allocation*

It is unsafe to registerize a variable if the eliminated memory access has some important side effect or visibility outside of the code under consideration. Examples of variables that should not be registerized include:

- Global variables shared between multiple functions or modules.

- Variables used as communication between concurrent threads.

- Variables accessed asynchronously by interrupt handlers.

- Variables used as memory-mapped I/O regions.

Note that some of these cases are more difficult to detect than others! Globally shared variables are already known to the compiler, but the other three cases are (often) not reflected in the language itself. In the C language, one can mark a variable with the `volatile` keyword to indicate that it may be changed by some method unknown to the compiler, and therefore clever optimizations should not be undertaken. Low level code found in operating systems or parallel programs is often compiled without such optimizations, so as to avoid these problems.

12.5.2 Priority of Register Allocation

For a small function, it may be possible to registerize *all* the variables, so that memory is not used at all. But for even a moderately complex function (or a CPU that has few available registers) it is likely that the compiler must choose a limited number of variables to registerize.

Before automatic register allocation was developed, the programmer was responsible for identifying such variables manually. For example, in early C compilers, one could add the `register` keyword to a variable declaration, forcing it to be stored in a register. This was typically done for the index variable of the inner-most loop. Of course, the programmer might not choose the best variable, or they might choose too many register variables, leaving too few available for temporaries. Today, the `register` keyword is essentially ignored by C compilers, which are capable of making informed decisions.

What strategy should we use to automatically pick variables to registerize? Naturally, those that experience the most number of loads and stores as the program runs. One could profile an execution of the program, count the memory accesses per variable, and then go back and select the top n variables. Of course, that would be a very slow and expensive procedure for optimizing a program, but one might conceivably go about it for a very performance-critical program.

A more reasonable approach would be to score variables via static analysis with some simple heuristics. In a linear sequence of code, each variable can be directly scored by the number of loads and stores it performs: the variable with the highest score is the best candidate. However, a variable access that appears inside a loop is likely to have a much higher access count. How large, we cannot say, but we can assume that a loop (and each nesting of a loop) multiplies the importance of a variable by a large constant. Multiply-nested loops increase importance in the same way.

12.5.3 Conflicts Between Variables

Not every variable needs a distinct register. Two variables can be assigned to the same register if their uses do not conflict. To determine this, we must first compute the **live ranges** of each variable and then construct a conflict graph. Within a basic block of a linear IR, a variable is live from its first definition until its final use. (If the same code is expressed in SSA form, then each version of a variable can be treated independently, with its own live range.)

Now, each variable with an overlapping range cannot share the same register, because they must exist independently. Conversely, two variables that do not have an overlapping live range can be assigned the same variable. We can construct a **conflict graph** where each node in the graph represents a variable, and then add edges between nodes whose live ranges overlap. Figure 12.5 gives an example of a conflict graph.

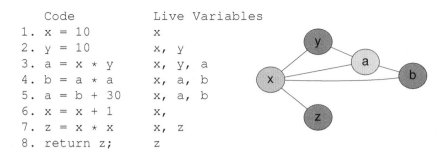

```
     Code                Live Variables
1.  x = 10               x
2.  y = 10               x, y
3.  a = x * y            x, y, a
4.  b = a * a            x, a, b
5.  a = b + 30           x, a, b
6.  x = x + 1            x,
7.  z = x * x            x, z
8.  return z;            z
```

Figure 12.5: Live Ranges and Register Conflict Graph

Register allocation now becomes an instance of the **graph coloring** problem. [7] The goal is to assign each node in the graph a different color (register) such that no two adjacent nodes have the same color. A planar graph (like a two-dimensional political map) can always be colored with four colors. [4] However, a register conflict graph is not necessarily planar, and so may require a large number of colors. The general problem of finding the minimum number of colors needed is NP-complete, but there are a number of simpler heuristics that are effective in practice.

A common approach is to sort the nodes of the graph by the number of edges (conflicts), and then assign registers to the most conflicted node first. Then, proceeding down the list, assign each node a register that is not already taken by an adjacent node. If at any point, the number of available registers is exhausted, then mark that node as a non-registerized variable, and continue, because it may be still possible to assign registers to nodes with fewer conflicts.

12.5.4   Global Register Allocation

The procedure above describes the analysis of live variables and register allocation for individual basic blocks. However, if each basic block is allocated independently, it would be very difficult to combine basic blocks, because variables would be assigned to different registers, or none at all.

---

[4]This mathematical problem has a particularly colorful (ahem) history. In 1852, Francis Guthrie conjectured that only four colors were necessary to color a planar graph, while attempting to color a map of Europe. He brought this problem to Augustus DeMorgan, who popularized it, leading to several other mathematicians who published several (incorrect) proofs in the late 1800s. In 1891, Percy John Heawood proved that no more than *five* colors were sufficient, and that's where things stood for the next 85 years. In 1976, Kenneth Appel and Wolfgang Haken produced a computer-assisted proof of the four-color theorem, but the proof contained over 400 pages of case-by-case analysis which had to be painstakingly verified by hand. This caused consternation in the mathematical community, partly due to the practical difficulty of verifying such a result, but also because this proof was unlike any that had come before. Does it really count as a "proof" if it cannot be easily contemplated and verified by a human? [2]

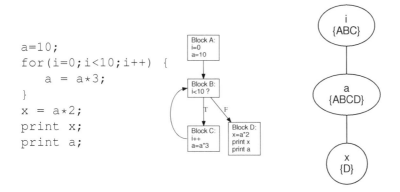

Figure 12.6: Example of Global Register Allocation

To perform register allocation on code (left) consisting of more than a basic block, build the control flow graph (middle) and then determine the blocks in which a given variable is live. Construct a conflict graph (right) such that variables sharing a live block are in conflict, and then color the graph.

It would become necessary to introduce code between each basic block to move variables between registers or to/from memory, which could defeat the benefits of allocation in the first place.

In order to perform global register allocation across an entire function body, we must do so in a way that keeps assignments consistent, no matter where the control flow leads. To do this, we first construct the control flow graph for the function. For each variable definition in the graph, trace the possible forward paths to uses of that variable, taking into account multiple paths made possible by loops and branches. If there exists a path from definition to use, then all the basic blocks in that path are members of the set of live basic blocks for that variable. Finally, a conflict graph may be constructed based on the sets of live blocks: each node represents a variable and its set of live basic blocks; each edge represents a conflict between two variables whose live sets intersect. (As above, the same analysis can be performed in SSA form for a more fine-grained register assignment.) Figure 12.6 gives an example of this analysis for a simple code fragment.

12.6   Optimization Pitfalls

Now that you have seen some common optimization techniques, you should be aware of some pitfalls common to all techniques.

Be careful of the correctness of optimizations. A given piece of code must produce the same result before and after optimization, for all possible inputs. We must be particularly careful with the boundary conditions of a given piece of code, where inputs are particularly large, or small, or run into fundamental limitations of the machine. These concerns require careful attention, particularly when applying general mathematical or logical observations to concrete code.

For example, it is tempting to apply common algebraic transformations to arithmetic expressions. We might transform `a/x + b/x` into `(a+b)/x` because these expressions are equal in the abstract world of real numbers.

Unfortunately, these two expressions are *not* the same in the concrete world of limited-precision mathematics. Suppose that a, b, and x are 32-bit signed integers, with a range of $[-2^31, +2^31)$. If both a and b have the value 2,000,000,000, then `a/5` is 400,000,000 and `a/5+b/5` is 800,000,000. However, `a+b` overflows a 32-bit register and wraps around to a negative value, so that `(a+b)/5` is -58993459! An optimizing compiler must be extremely cautious that any code transformations produce the same results under *all possible values* in the program.

Be careful not to change external side-effects. Many aspects of real programs depend upon the side-effects, not the results of a computation. This is most apparent in embedded systems and hardware drivers, where an operating system or an application communicates with external devices through memory-mapped registers. But, it is also the case in conventional user-mode programs that may perform I/O or other forms of communication via system calls: a `write()` system call should never be eliminated by an optimization. Unfortunately, positively identifying every external function that has side effects is impractical. An optimizing compiler must conservatively assume that any external function *might* have a side effect, and leave it untouched.

Be careful of how optimization changes debugging. A program compiled with aggressive optimizations can show surprising behavior when run under a debugger. Statements may be executed in a completely different order than stated in the program, giving the impression that the program flow jumps forwards and backwards without explanation. Entire parts of the program may be skipped entirely, if they are determined to be unreachable, or have been simplified away. Variables mentioned in the source might not exist in the executable at all. Breakpoints set on function calls may never be reached, if the function has been inlined. In short, many of the things observable by a debugger are not really program results, but hidden internal state and are not guaranteed to appear in the final executable program. If you expect your program to have bugs – and it will – better fix them before enabling optimizations.

12.7 Optimization Interactions

Multiple optimizations can interact with each other in ways that are unpredictable. Sometimes, these interactions cascade in positive ways: constant folding can support reachability analysis, resulting in dead code elimination. On the other hand, optimizations can interact in negative ways: function inlining can result in more complex expressions, resulting in less efficient register allocation. What's worse is that one set of optimizations may be very effective on one program, but counter productive on another.

A modern optimizing compiler can easily have fifty different optimization techniques of varying complexity. If it is only a question of turning each optimization on or off, then there are (only) 2^{50} combinations. But, if the optimizations can be applied in any order, there are $fact(50)$ permutations! How is the user to decide which optimizations to enable?

Most production compilers define a few discrete levels of optimization. For example, gcc defines -O0 as the fastest compile speed, with no optimization, -O1 enables about thirty optimizations with modest compile-time expense and few runtime drawbacks (e.g. dead code elimination), -O2 enables another thirty optimizations with greater compile-time expense (e.g. code hoisting), and -O3 enables aggressive optimizations that may or may not pay off (e.g. loop unrolling.) On top of that, individual optimizations may be turned on or off manually.

But is it possible to do better with finer-grained control? A number of researchers have explored methods of finding the best combinations of optimizations, given a benchmark program that runs reasonably quickly. For example, the CHiLL [8] framework combines parallel execution of benchmarks with a high level heuristic search algorithm to prune the overall search space. Another approach is to use genetic algorithms [9] in which a representative set of configurations is iteratively evaluated, mutated, recombined, until a strong configuration emerges.

12.8   Exercises

1. To get a good sense of the performance of your machine, follow the advice of Jon Bentley [1] and write some simple benchmarks to measure these fundamental operations:

   (a) Integer arithmetic.

   (b) Floating point arithmetic.

   (c) Array element access.

   (d) A simple function call.

   (e) A memory allocation.

   (f) A system call like open().

2. Obtain a standard set of benchmark codes (such as SPEC) and evaluate the effect of various optimization flags available on your favorite compiler.

3. Implement the constant folding optimization in the AST of your project compiler.

4. Identify three opportunities for strength reduction in the B-Minorlanguage and implement them in your project compiler.

5. Implement reachability analysis in your project compiler, using either the AST or a CFG. Use this to ensure that all flow control paths through a function end in a suitable return statement.

6. Write code to compute and display the live ranges of all variables used in your project compiler.

7. Implement linear-scan register allocation [6] on basic blocks, based on the live ranges computed in the previous exercise.

8. Implement graph-coloring register allocation [7] on basic blocks, based on the live ranges computed in the previous exercise.

12.9 Further Reading

1. J. Bentley, "Programming Pearls", Addison-Wesley, 1999.
   A timeless book that offers the programmer a variety of strategies for evaluating the performance of a program and improving its algorithms and data structures.

2. R. Wilson, "Four Colors Suffice: How the Map Problem Was Solved", Princeton University Press, 2013.
   A history of the long winding road from the four-color conjecture in the nineteenth century to its proof by computer in the twentieth century.

3. A. Aho, M. S. Lam, R. Sethi, J. D. Ullman, "Compilers: Principles, Techniques, and Tools", 2nd edition, Pearson, 2013.
   Affectionally known as the "Dragon Book", this is an advanced and comprehensive book on optimizing compilers, and you are now ready to tackle it.

4. S. L. Graham, P. B. Kessler, and M. K. McKusick. "Gprof: A call graph execution profiler." ACM SIGPLAN Notices, volume 17, number 6, 1982. https://doi.org/10.1145/872726.806987

5. A. Aho, M. Ganapathi, and S. Tjiang, "Code Generation Using Tree Matching and Dynamic Programming", ACM Transactions on Programming Languages and Systems, volume 11, number 4, 1989. https://doi.org/10.1145/69558.75700

6. M. Poletto and V. Sarkar, "Linear Scan Register Allocation", ACM Transactions on Programming Languages and Systems, volume 21, issue 5, 1999. https://doi.org/10.1145/330249.330250

7. G. J. Chaitin, "Register Allocation & Spilling via Graph Coloring", ACM SIGPLAN Notices, voume 17, issue 6, June 1982.
   https://doi.org/10.1145/800230.806984

8. A. Tiwari, C. Chen, J. Chame, M. Hall, J. Hollingsworth, "A Scalable Auto-tuning framework for compiler optimization", IEEE International Symposium on Parallel and Distributed Processing, 2009.
   https://doi.org/10.1109/IPDPS.2009.5161054

9. M. Stephenson, S. Amarasinghe, M. Martin, U. O'Reilly, "Meta optimization: improving compiler heuristics with machine learning", ACM SIGPLAN Conference on Programming Language Design and Implementation, 2003.
   https://doi.org/10.1145/781131.781141

Appendix A – Sample Course Project

This appendix describes a semester-long course project which is the suggested companion to this book. Your instructor may decide to use it as-is, or make some modifications appropriate to the time and place of your class. The overall goal of the project is to build a complete compiler that accepts a high level language as input and produces working assembly code as output. It can naturally be broken down into several stages, each one due at an interval of a few weeks, allowing for 4-6 assignmnets over the course of a semester.

The recommended project is to use the B-Minor language as the source, and X86 or ARM assembly as the output, since both are described in this book. But you could accomplish similar goals with a different source language (like C, Pascal, or Rust) or a different assembly language or intermediate representation (like MIPS, JVM, or LLVM.)

Naturally, the stages are cumulative: the parser cannot work correctly unless the scanner works correctly, so it is important for you to get each one right, before moving onto the next one. A critical development technique is to create a large number (30 or more) test cases for each stage, and provide a script or some other automated means for running them automatically. This will give you confidence that the compiler works across all the different aspects of B-Minor, and that a fix to one problem doesn't break something else.

A.1 Scanner Assignment

Construct a scanner for B-Minor which reads in a source file and produces a listing of each token one by one, annotated with the token kind (identifier, integer, string, etc) and the location in the source. If invalid input is discovered, produce a message, recover from the error, and continue. Create a set of complete tests to exercise all of the tricky corner cases of comments, strings, escape characters, and so forth.

A.2 Parser Assignment

Building on the scanner, construct a parser for B-Minor using Bison (or another appropriate tool) which reads in a source file and determines whether the grammar is valid, and indicates success or failure. Use the diagnostic features of Bison to evaluate the given grammar for ambiguities and work to resolve problems such as the dangling-else. Create a set of complete tests to exercise all of the tricky corner cases.

A.3 Pretty-Printer Assignment

Next, use the parser to construct the complete AST for the source program. To verify the correctness of the AST, print it back out in as an equivalent source program, but with all of the whitespace arranged nicely so that it is pleasant to read. This will result in some interesting discussions with the instructor about what constitutes an "equivalent" program. A necessary (but not sufficient) requirement is that the output program should be re-parseable by the same tool. This requires attention to some details with comments, strings, and general formatting. Again, create a set of test cases.

A.4 Typechecker Assignment

Next, add methods which walk the AST and perform semantic analysis to determine the correctness of the program. Symbol references must be resolved to definitions, the type of expressions must be inferred, and the compatibility of values in context must be checked. You are probably used to encountering incomprehensible error messages from compilers: this is your opportunity to improve upon the situation. Again, create a set of test cases.

A.5 Optional: Intermediate Representation

Optionally, the project can be extended by adding a pass to convert the AST into an intermediate representation. This could be a custom three or four-tuple code, an internal DAG, or a well established IR such as JVM or LLVM. The advantage of using the later is that output can be easily fed into existing tools and actually executed, which should give you some satisfaction. Again, create a set of test cases.

A.6 Code Generator Assignment

The most exciting step is to finally emit working assembly code. Straightforward code generation is most easily performed on the AST itself, or a DAG derived from the AST in the optional IR assignment, following the procedure in Chapter 11. For the first attempt, it's best not to be concerned about the efficiency of the code, but allow each code block to conservatively stand on its own. It is best to start with some extremely simple programs (e.g. `return 2+2;`) and gradually add complexity bit by bit. Here, your practice in constructing test cases will really pay off, because you will be able to quickly verify how many test programs are affected by one change to the compiler.

A.7 Optional: Extend the Language

In the final step, you are encouraged to develop your own ideas for extending B-Minor itself with new data types or control structures, to create a new backend targeting a different CPU architecture, or to implement one or more optimizations described in Chapter 12.

Appendix B – The B-Minor Language

B.1 Overview

The B-Minor language is a "little" language suitable for use in an undegraduate compilers class. B-Minor includes expressions, basic control flow, recursive functions, and strict type checking. It is object-code compatible with ordinary C and thus can take advantage of the standard C library, within its defined types.

B-Minor is similar enough to C that it should feel familiar, but has enough variations to allow for some discussion of different language choices affect the implementation. For example, the type syntax of B-Minor is closer to that of Pascal or SQL than of C. Students may find this awkward at first, but its value becomes clearer when constructing a parser and when discussing types independently of the symbols that they apply to. The `print` statement gives an opportunity to perform simple type inference and interact with runtime support. A few unusual operators cannot be implemented in a single assembly instruction, illustrating how complex language intrinsics are implemented. The strict type system gives the students some experience with reasoning about rigorous type algebras and producing detailed error messages.

A proper language definition would be quite formal, including regular expressions for each token type, a context-free-grammar, a type algebra, and so forth. However, if we provided all that detail, it would rob you (the student) of the valuable experience of wrestling with those details. Instead, we will describe the language through examples, leaving it to you to read carefully, and then extract the formal specifications needed for your code. You are certain to find some details and corner cases that are unclear or incompletely specified. Use that as an opportunity to ask questions during class or office hours and work towards a more precise specification.

B.2   Tokens

In B-Minor , whitespace is any combination of the following characters: tabs, spaces, linefeed, and carriage return. The placement of whitespace is not significant in B-Minor . Both C-style and C++-style comments are valid in B-Minor :

```
/* A C-style comment */
a=5; // A C++ style comment
```

Identifiers (i.e. variable and function names) may contain letters, numbers, and underscores. Identifiers must begin with a letter or an underscore. These are examples of valid identifiers:

```
i x mystr fog123 BigLongName55
```

The following strings are B-Minor keywords and may not be used as identifiers:

```
array boolean char else false for function if
integer print return string true void while
```

B.3   Types

B-Minor has four atomic types: integers, booleans, characters, and strings. A variable is declared as a name followed by a colon, then a type and an optional initializer. For example:

```
x: integer;
y: integer = 123;
b: boolean = false;
c: char    = 'q';
s: string  = "hello world\n";
```

An integer is always a signed 64 bit value. boolean can take the literal values true or false. char is a single 8-bit ASCII character. string is a double-quoted constant string that is null-terminated and cannot be modified. (Note that, unlike C, string is not an array of char, it is a completely separate type.)

Both char and string may contain the following backslash codes. n indicates a linefeed (ASCII value 10), 0 indicates a null (ASCII value zero), and a backslash followed by anything else indicates exactly the following character. Both strings and identifiers may be up to 256 characters long. ¡p¿ B-Minor also allows arrays of a fixed size. They may be declared with no value, which causes them to contain all zeros:

```
a: array [5] integer;
```

Or, the entire array may be given specific values:

```
a: array [5] integer = {1,2,3,4,5};
```

B.4   Expressions

B-Minor has many of the arithmetic operators found in C, with the same meaning and level of precedence:

`[]  f()`	array subscript, function call
`++  --`	postfix increment, decrement
`-  !`	unary negation, logical not
`^`	exponentiation
`*  /  %`	multiplication, division, modulus
`+  -`	addition, subtraction
`<  <=  >  >=  ==  !=`	comparison
`&&  ||`	logical and, logical or
`=`	assignment

B-Minor is *strictly typed*. This means that you may only assign a value to a variable (or function parameter) if the types match *exactly*. You cannot perform many of the fast-and-loose conversions found in C. For example, arithmetic operators can only apply to integers. Comparisons can be performed on arguments of any type, but only if they match. Logical operations can only be performed on booleans.

Following are examples of some (but not all) type errors:

```
x: integer = 65;
y: char = 'A';
if(x>y) ... // error: x and y are of different types!

f: integer = 0;
if(f) ...        // error: f is not a boolean!

writechar: function void ( char c );
a: integer = 65;
writechar(a);   // error: a is not a char!

b: array [2] boolean = {true,false};
x: integer = 0;
x = b[0];       // error: x is not a boolean!
```

Following are some (but not all) examples of correct type assignments:

```
b: boolean;
x: integer = 3;
y: integer = 5;
b = x<y;        // ok: the expression x<y is boolean

f: integer = 0;
```

```
if(f==0) ...      // ok: f==0 is a boolean expression

c: char = 'a';
if(c=='a') ...   // ok: c and 'a' are both chars
```

B.5 Declarations and Statements

In B-Minor , you may declare global variables with optional constant initializers, function prototypes, and function definitions. Within functions, you may declare local variables (including arrays) with optional initialization expressions. Scoping rules are identical to C. Function definitions may not be nested.

Within functions, basic statements may be arithmetic expressions, `return` statements, `print` statements, `if` and `if-else` statements, `for` loops, or code within inner   groups. B-Minor does not have switch statements, while-loops, or do-while loops, since those are easily represented as special cases of `for` and `if`.

The `print` statement is a little unusual because it is a statement and not a function call. `print` takes a list of expressions separated by commas, and prints each out to the console, like this:

```
print "The temperature is: ", temp, " degrees\n";
```

Note that each element in the list following a `print` statement is an expression of *any* type. The `print` mechanism will automatically infer the type and print out the proper representation.

B.6 Functions

Functions are declared in the same way as variables, except giving a type of `function` followed by the return type, arguments, and code:

```
square: function integer ( x: integer ) = {
    return x^2;
}
```

The return type of a function must be one of the four atomic types, or `void` to indicate no type. Function arguments may be of any type. `integer`, `boolean`, and `char` arguments are passed by value, while `string` and `array` arguments are passed by reference. As in C, arrays passed by reference have an indeterminate size, and so the length is typically passed as an extra argument:

```
printarray: function void
  ( a: array [] integer, size: integer ) = {
    i: integer;
    for( i=0;i<;size;i++) {
        print a[i], "\n";
    }
}
```

A function prototype states the existence and type of the function, but includes no code. This must be done if the user wishes to call an external function linked by another library. For example, to invoke the C function puts:

```
puts: function void ( s: string );

main: function integer () = {
    puts("hello world");
}
```

A complete program must have a main function that returns an integer. the arguments to main may either be empty, or use argc and argv in the same manner as C. (The declaration of argc and argv is left as an exercise to the reader.)

B.7   Optional Elements

Creating a complete implementation of the language above from beginning to end should be more than enough to keep a undergraduate class busy for a semester. However, if you need some additional challenge, consider the following ideas:

- Add a new native type complex which implements complex numbers. To make this useful, you will need to add some additional functions or operators to construct complex values, perform arithmetic, and extract the real and imaginary parts.

- Add a new automatic type var which allows one to declare a variable without a concrete type. The compiler should infer the type automatically based on assignments made to that variable. Consider carefully what should happen if a function definition has a parameter of type var.

- Improve the safety of arrays by making the array accesses automatically checked at runtime against the known size of the array. This requires making the length of the array a runtime property stored in memory alongside the array data, checking each array access against the boundaries, and taking appropriate action on a violation. Compare the performance of checked arrays against unchecked arrays. (The X86 BOUND instruction might be helpful.)

- Add a new mutable string type `mutstring` which has a fixed size, but can be modified in place, and can be converted to and from a regular `string` as needed.

- Add an alternative control flow structure like `switch`, which evaluates a single control expression, and then branches to alternatives with matching values. For an extra challenge, allow `switch` to select value ranges, not just constant values.

- Implement structure types that allow multiple data items to be grouped together in a simple type. At the assembly level, this is not very different from implementing arrays, because each element is simply at a known offset from the base object. However, parsing and typechecking become more complicated because the elements associated with a structure type must be tracked.

Appendix C – Coding Conventions

C has been the language of choice for implementing low level systems like compilers, operating systems, and drivers since the 1980s. However, it is fair to say that C does not enforce a wide variety of good programming practices, in comparison to other languages. To write solid C, you need to exercise a high degree of self-discipline. [1]

For many students, a compilers course in college is the first place where you are asked to create a good sized piece of software, refining it through several development cycles until the final project is reached. This is a good opportunity for you to pick up some good habits that will make you more productive.

To that end, here are the coding conventions that I ask my students to observe when writing C code. Each of these recommendations requires a little more work up front, but will save you headaches in the long run.

Use a version control system. There are a variety of nice open source systems for keeping track of your source code. Today, Git, Mercurial, and Subversion are quite popular, and I'm sure next year will bring a new one. Pick one, learn the basic features, and shape your code gradually by making small commits.[2]

Go from working to working. Never leave your code in a broken state. Begin by checking in the simplest possible sketch of your program that compiles and works, even if it only prints out "hello world". Then, add to the program in a minor way, make sure that it compiles and runs, and check it in. [3]

Eliminate dead code. Students often pick up the habit of commenting out one bit of code while they attempt to change it and test it. While this is

---

[1] Why not use C++ to address some of these disciplines? Although C++ is a common part of many computer science curricula, I generally discourage the use of C++ by students. Although it has many features that are attractive at first glance, they are not powerful enough to allow you to dispense with the basic C mechanisms. (For example, even if you use the C++ string class, you still need to understand basic character arrays and pointers.) Further, the language is so complex that very few people really understand the complete set of features and how they interact. If you stick with C, what you see is what you get.

[2] Some people like to spend endless hours arguing about the proper way to use arcane features of these tools. Don't be one of those people: learn the basic operations and spend your mental energy on your code instead.

[3] This advice is often attributed as one of Jim Gray's "Laws of Data Engineering" in slide presentations, but I haven't been able to find an authoratative reference.

a reasonable tactic to use for a quick test, don't allow this dead code to pile up in your program, otherwise your source code will quickly become incomprehensible. Remove unused code, data, comments, files, or anything else that is unnecessary to the program, so that you can clearly see what it does now. Trust your version control system to allow you to go back to a previously working version, if needed.

Use tools to handle indenting. Don't waste your time arguing about indenting style; find a tool that does it for you automatically, and then forget about it. Your editor probably has a mode to indent automatically. If not, use the standard Unix tool `indent`.

Name things consistently. In this book, you will see that every function consists of a noun and a verb: `expr_typecheck`, `decl_codegen`, etc. Each one is used consistently: `expr` is always used for expressions, `codegen` is always used for code generation. Every function dealing with expressions is in the `expr` module. It may be tempting to take shortcuts or make abbreviations in the heat of battle, but this will come back to bite you. Do it right the first time.

Put only the interface in a header file. In C, a header file (like `expr.h`) is used to describe the elements needed to call a function: function prototypes and the types and constants necessary to invoke those functions. If a function is only used within one module, it should *not* be mentioned in the header file, because nobody outside the module needs that information.

Put only the implementation in a source file. In C, a source file (like `expr.c`) is used to provide the definitions of functions. In the source file, you should include the correpsonding header (`expr.h`) so that the compiler can check that your function definitions match the prototypes. Any function or variable that is private to the module should be declared `static`.

Be lazy and recursive. Many language data structures are hierarchically nested. When designing an algorithm, take note of the nested data structures, and pass responsibility to other functions, even if you haven't written them yet. This technique generally results in code that is simple, compact, and readable. For example, to print out a variable declaration, break it down into printing the name, then the type, then the value, with some punctuation in between:

```
printf("%s:\n",d->name);
type_print(d->type);
printf(" = ");
expr_print(d->value);
printf(" ;\n");
```

Then proceed to writing `type_print` and `expr_print`, if you haven't done them already.

Use a Makefile to build everything automatically. Learn how to write a Makefile, if you haven't already. The basic syntax of Make is very simple.

The following rule says that `expr.o` depends upon `expr.c` and `expr.h`, and can be built by running the command `gcc`:

```
expr.o: expr.c expr.h
   gcc expr.c -c -o expr.o -Wall
```

There are many variations of Make that include wildcards, and pattern substitution, and all manner of other things that can be confusing to the uninitiated. Just start by writing plain old rules whose meaning is clear.

Null pointers are your friends. When designing a data structure, use null pointers to indicate when nothing is present. You cannot derefence a null pointer, of course, and so you must check before using it. This can lead to code cluttered with null checks everywhere, like this:

```
void expr_codegen( struct expr *e, FILE *output )
{
    if(e->left) expr_codegen(e->left,output);
    if(e->right) expr_codegen(e->right,output);


    . . .

}
```

You can eliminate many of them by simply placing the check at the beginning of the function, and programming in a recursive style:

```
void expr_codegen( struct expr *e, FILE *output )
{
    if(!e) return;

    expr_codegen(e->left,output);
    expr_codegen(e->right,output);


    . . .

}
```

Automate regression testing. A compiler has to handle a large number of details, and it is all to easy for you to accidentally introduce a new bug when attempting to fix an old one. To handle this, create a simple test suite that consists of a set of sample programs, some correct and some incorrect. Write a little script that invokes your compiler on each sample program, and makes sure that it succeeds for the good tests, and fails on the bad tests. Make it a part of your Makefile, so that every time you touch the code, the tests are run, and you will know if things are still working.

Index

Made in the USA
Columbia, SC
22 December 2020